Tea Treasures

...and More

By Carol Sims

FAVORITE RECIPES FROM
SIMS & COMPANY

Copyright © 2003
by
Carol Sims

ISBN: 0-9742985-0-6

First Printing
September 2003

Photography of Sims boys 2003: Jennifer Sparks Harriman
Special thanks to John Bibee for his editing expertise.

For information on tea or tea accoutrements
or to order *Tea Treasures and More*, call
512-330-9991, 512-327-3782, or visit our website at
www.teatreasures.com
a taste of elegance with efficiency

Tea Treasures
2406 Rollingwood Drive
Austin, TX 78746

Proverbs 2:4-5

Designer Series
Wimmer Cookbooks

Table of Contents

Tea Treasures and More

~ 1988 ~

To my family's future generation, I dedicate these treasures of tea and cuisine. Ryan, Jonathan, and Benjamin—all born and raised to adulthood in Austin, Texas, enjoyed themselves in this gourmet "fertile crescent." We always felt access to more good restaurants at better prices than any other place in the world. At home, however, I passed the excellent kitchen craft and hospitality of my southern mother to our table. I was rewarded with a family of connoisseurs who enjoyed and encouraged my cooking endeavors and three sons who are surpassing me in their own cookery. My southern roots of growing up in Atlanta, Georgia are deep in my soul along with my northern father, born of German immigrants, who contributed to the memory of my palate during my childhood years in Ridgewood, New Jersey. Both experiences enriched my life and inspired the volume in your hand. For this eclectic assortment of favorites, I thank my family and friends, especially my husband Bob.

Carol Eidschun Sims

Photographer: Jennifer Sparks Harriman

~ Ryan, Ben, Jonathan 2003 ~

4

Tea Treasures

As James Norwood Pratt says, "Tea is a treasure to the world." Since tea is one of the treasures I've discovered over my lifetime, it stole prominence as the lead chapter of this cookbook! We usually have to search for treasures, and they are often unexpected. In addition to my spiritual blessings and my family, tea has been one of those delightful surprises. In fact, out of that discovery evolved my business **Tea Treasures**.

My business card constantly amuses me and opens a subculture to others. One of the most fun things I do is wait for their response after reading it— "What is a tea consultant? How did you get involved in the tea business?" Truthfully, the tea business seduced me. I've been drinking tea since I was in college. As a child, my mother would reward me with a teaspoon of her coffee in my milk, so it was surprising when I became old enough, I didn't like coffee. In fact, I have never had a whole cup of coffee. I have to admit I used to be jealous of my coffee-drinking friends, because they seemed to enjoy their gourmet coffee and expressed so much delight in it. Since becoming more educated about tea and experiencing finer teas, I'm no longer jealous; in fact, my tea ritual rewards with simple and great pleasure.

Tea is not only a source of nourishment but also a reassuring presence to a relational world. As Emily Barnes says in *If Teacups Could Talk*, *it's not the tea that makes teatime special, it's the spirit of the tea party. It's what happens when women or men or children make a place in their life for the rituals of sharing. It's what happens when we bother with the little extras that feed the soul and nurture the senses and make space for unhurried conversation. And when that happens, it doesn't really matter what fills the cups or holds the liquid.*

Teatime helps us to make room for stillness in our lives, reducing residual stress and physical tension. The act of making and serving tea forces us to slow down, relax, and become civilized. I enjoy solitary tea times in front of a fire, on a terrace in the morning sun, with a good novel or with Scripture during a quiet time with God—a Sunday afternoon with a family member or friend, an elaborate formal tea party, or the routine afternoon tea break at my office. I joyfully anticipate the event. There is a hopeful element involved in drinking tea—as Gail Greco says, *Somehow, taking tea together encourages an atmosphere of intimacy when you slip off the timepiece in your mind and cast your fate to a delight of tasty tea, tiny foods, and thoughtful conversation.*

Tea Treasures

Drinking tea is a discovery of a lifetime, a hobby similar to wine drinking, yet remarkably more approachable—not only in searching for your favorite teas but also the accoutrements and ceremony that go along with it. I love beautiful antique teapots with decorative porcelain teacups, unique silver spoons, and, of course, the delicious food that make an afternoon tea memorable. There are times I enjoy the serenity of a simple Asian Yixing clay pot or a German glass teapot. My fifty percent German heritage insists that my tea accoutrements work well, so evolved Tea Treasures's philosophy, *an engaging, elegant, and efficient way to serve tea.* In this section about tea, I'll be sharing my favorites emerging from three decades of practice.

Buying and Storing Tea

Tea absorbs flavors, odors and moisture easily, all to its ruin. Freezing will not work. Light will destroy it, too. So, practically, put it in the tightest, darkest, driest containers that contain no residue from former "occupants." An example of what does not work: I found some of the best (before it was put into the grocery store) quality Keemun displayed in bulk in a clear jar that formerly contained Earl Grey tea. The oil of bergamot residue altered the flavor dramatically, and the fluorescent lights in the store added the death-blow. The tea was awful. This was an upscale health food store. It gets worse. If coffee is stored or handled near tea, that will also ruin the taste. Coffee residue is another of the many strong oils that are almost impossible to remove from containers, so get tea canisters that have double airtight lids and avoid plastic. Tea bought in a store might be a year old. Tea can now be purchased from vendors like **teatreasures.com** that was picked eight weeks before it was delivered. Nearly anyone can taste the difference.

The Agony of the Leaves

Most people enjoy and know more about the ritual and décor of tea drinking than about the heart of it all—the tea. Learning about tea definitely enhanced my enjoyment of the daily celebration. There is so much to learn, that I will only share some tidbits. Basically all true teas (not herbal or fruit infusions) come from the leaves or buds of the *Camellia sinensis* (also called *Thea sinensis*) plant. The more than 3,000 categories of tea are divided into five general types: white, green, oolong, black, Pu-erh and flavored. What makes them so different in taste, aroma, and appearance is where they are grown—the soil, altitude, climate—and how they are processed.

White teas are rare and expensive, processed the least amount of time, mostly found in the Fujian Province of China and brew almost colorless with a delicate flavor.

Green teas are freshly plucked leaves, which are steamed or heated for only several minutes to half the oxidizing process. Then the leaves are dried by machine or hand and rolled into a number of styles—balled, flat, curly, thin, or twisted.

Oolong teas have a withering and oxidation process much shorter than black teas but longer than green teas. They share some taste and characteristics of both black and green. The oolong process adds complexity and time to this type, often reflected in the price. Formosa Oolong reflects leaves dried in the sun versus heated sheds and produces remarkably vibrant aroma.

Black teas are fresh, green leaves, which are first withered after picking, spread out to dry, then crushed by rollers to release the juices. This oxidation process turns the leaves brown. Then they are fired by hot air to dry. The *orthodox method* of processing twists and breaks the leaf but doesn't cut it into small pieces. The *CTC method* of cutting, tearing, and curling chops the tea by machine into tiny particles, which causes the tea to brew quickly for a stronger infusion (meaning less tea used). Most teabags use CTC tea. The last part of the process is the sorting and grading of the tea. Black tea became very popular in western culture, because of longer shelf-life, as the clipper ships took many months to transport tea from Asia to Europe.

Pu-erh, the name of a city in Yunnan near the place tea was discovered in China, is also the name for an entire class of tea by that name. The Pu-erh name means the tea was oxidized twice. There is a bit of mystery surrounding Pu-erh, as it is the only tea that seems to improve with age. I drank some this year that was twenty years old. Typically it is dark, and the infusion is black and "thick." A friend from Singapore, who loved its tradition for overall health qualities, especially aiding digestion, introduced me to this tea. The taste is acquired and very earthy and "indefinably different." If it tastes moldy or smells of mildew, it is. Good Pu-erh is never moldy.

Flavored teas have become more and more popular. They vary from green to black flavored with dried fruit, flowers, herbs, oils, candy, and spices. The word tea is often used for other herbal infusions, which are not the *camellia sinensis* plant. Now becoming more and more popular in the U.S. are **Rooibos** from South Africa, **Yerba Mate** from South America, and **Lemon Myrtle** from Australia.

The black teas most common to Westerners are imported from China (Keemun and Yunnan), India (Assam and Darjeeling), and Sri Lanka (Ceylon). Display teas are mostly green teas (from China) hand-crafted to open up into beautiful ornaments when brewed and fun to view in glass teapots or to enjoy with desserts.

The lowest quality tea in the world is usually grown in Argentina, ground into dust and manufactured and sold to Americans in chlorine-bleached teabags in the grocery store. I encourage you to begin brewing loose tea. Many fine teas and blends can be found in the U.S. at gourmet stores, tearooms, catalogs, or online (teatreasures.com). Almost anyone can afford to be a tea connoisseur. Tea (as wine) has 95 percent of the complete palate of humans without added flavors. At 200 cups and often more per pound, the finest teas in the world are cheaper per cup than a cup of coffee at trendy "Arabica" coffee shops.

The important thing to remember about tea drinking is there's not a right or wrong tea to drink. It's all personal taste. There are preferable brewing techniques and recommendations of pairing different teas to certain foods, but the choice is all yours; and the discovery of your favorites will grow with time. It's amazing how I can prepare the same tea the same way every morning, but some days, it just tastes better. There are many methods of how to brew tea. Here is the Sims version:

How to Brew a Pot of Tea Properly

1. Boil a kettle of freshly drawn water. The water you use will have a definite affect on the taste of your tea. *All water is not created equal.* We filter our water before we boil it. (My favorite kettles are electric which automatically turn off when the water reaches boiling temperature 212°.) The higher the oxygen content the better, so don't over boil your water. Black teas should be brewed with boiling water, but green teas need lower temperatures. Many Westerners don't like green tea because they've brewed it too hot and too long. Helen Gustafson has a wonderful book *The Green Tea User's Manual* where she explains Chinese scholars define stages in the boiling of water which will help you: **Fish Eyes** (160°-180° F.)—pin-size bubbles ⅛-inch-diameter resembling the eyes of fish along with a faint hissing sound. **String of Pearls** (180°-190° F.) when bubbles break the surface or

8

begin to cling to the sides of the pan. **Turbulent Waters** (190°-210° F.) when large bubbles break the surface as a rolling boil. Most oolong teas brew well at "string of pearls" while more delicate green teas at "fish eyes" for two minutes, and black teas definitely at a "turbulent waters" for 3 to 5 minutes. Many aficionados prefer letting the full boil relinquish its power and brew at 203° for health and taste preference. Others insist on 212° water, but at high altitudes water boils at lower temperatures, and taste is affected. Experiment to your taste. I am the only aficionado present during my morning celebration! Most people will find their own way over time, and all develop a personal artistry.

2. Preheat the teapot and teacup by pouring some of the hot water into your pot and cup first—swirl it around and pour it out through the top or spout, to warm them both up.

3. Measure the tea using 1 teaspoon per person. You may put the tea directly into the pot or use an infuser, which we prefer with our Chatsford teapots. I prefer to use the same teaspoon every time. (Small versus heaping teaspoons may depend on how strong and large leaf the tea is as well as your personal taste.) You can be more accurate and consistent brewing your tea in smaller teapots (2-cup).

4. Add rapidly boiling water to the pot. Cover the pot and steep for 2 to 5 minutes, depending on how strong you like it. We use a digital timer. The moment the boiling water touches the tea has been called "the agony of the leaves." During the infusion, three things occur—1) "caffeine" (or teanine) comes out first. 2) Color comes next. 3) Flavor builds rapidly on the backend of the time. Tea leaves need enough room to unfurl and move about, and it's fun to view the tea as it moves around and does its thing.

5. When the brewing time is up, remove the infuser and pour into cups using a strainer if necessary. If there is tea left in the teapot, cover with your tea cozy to keep it hot for the next cup. For serving a large group of people, you may keep pouring boiling water into the pot several times over the infused leaves. (After the first pot, your tea is decaffeinated.) Then begin again with fresh leaves. (The used tea leaves are great to feed to your geraniums!) As John Harney says, *Boiling water is the key to everything. Without boiling water, you shouldn't have it. You shouldn't do it.* Of course, he's referring to black tea.

How to Decaffeinate Tea

About 80 percent or more of the tea's caffeine (technically called teanine) content is released within the first 30 seconds of steeping. You can enjoy all teas by decaffeinating the tea yourself by discarding the water after the first 30 seconds' steeping, then adding fresh boiling water to the remaining leaves. Some say tea has constituents which act to soothe and relax the body. These polyphenols begin to dissolve only in the third minute of steeping. This is the secret to bedtime tea. *If you are cold, tea will warm you; if you are heated, it will cool you. If you're depressed, it will cheer you. If you're excited, it will calm you.* —William Ewart Gladstone (1809-1898)

There is more caffeine in a pound of tea than in a pound of coffee. However, a pound of coffee produces about 40 cups, whereas a pound of tea produces about 200 cups. Green tea has about one-third as much caffeine as black tea, and oolong has about two-thirds as much. Therefore, on a per cup basis all tea has less "caffeine" than coffee.

Health Benefits of Tea

1. Tea is rich in disease-fighting antioxidants called polyphenols which can help prevent chronic diseases such as cancer, especially leukemia where DNA is actually repaired. Studies suggest a link between tea-drinking and a reduced risk of cancers, including stomach, skin, esophageal, and breast. (Green and oolong teas are preferred for cancers.)

2. Drinking tea may help protect the heart by relaxing the blood vessels, inhibiting blood clots, and improving blood-cholesterol levels. Polyphenols inhibit the angiotensin converting the enzyme that is known to cause hypertension.

3. Tea leaves have fluoride and phytoestrogens, which may increase bone density and guard against osteoporosis and tooth decay. Coffee depletes the calcium in the body, while tea helps you retain it.

4. Tea contains theraflavins and therarubignins that can help to relieve asthmatic and respiratory inflammations. It also has antibacterial properties that can inhibit staphylococcus and streptococcus infections.

5. Tea is a natural source of manganese, which aids the body's protein and energy metabolism. Tea is the only thing you can drink that can calm you and also give you energy at the same time.

6. Because of the powerful antioxidant qualities in tea, many cosmetic companies are using green tea concentrates in cosmetics and skincare products.

7. Three other herbal infusions that I'd like to mention are Rooibos from South Africa, Yerba Mate cultivated in Paraguay, and Lemon Myrtle from Australia. **Rooibos** (caffeine free) is rich in minerals and Vitamin C and has been popular among athletes because it has so much potassium, manganese, and sodium. Recent research in Japan shows it to have more antioxidants than green tea and helps people with disturbed sleeping patterns, stomach, and indigestive problems. I have personally experienced many of these benefits and especially enjoy the flavored Rooibos iced and hot. It would be a wonderful everyday drink for children.

8. **Yerba Mate** appeared among natives in Paraguay hundreds of years ago. It is now a cultural touchstone in South America. In addition to many other nutrients, it offers a combination of stimulants that are useful to most people. In fact, many people report better sleep, less fatigue and less desire to eat. Some say it acts like a tonic, stimulating a weakened and depressed nervous system and sedating an overexcited one, with increased resistance to both physical and mental fatigue. It's been reported to have positive effects on the gastrointestinal, cardiovascular, and immune systems. Mate also comes in different flavors and enjoyed cold or hot. In Paraguay and surrounding countries, it is called terrere when made cold.

9. **Lemon Myrtle** (the world's richest known natural source of citral) has a refreshing flavor and aroma of lemon grass, lime, and lemon and is grown organically in the rain forests of eastern Australia. It's known for its antibacterial, anti-viral, anti-fungal properties and calmative effects. We enjoy it hot just as it is, as well as using it as a spice in cooking. Citral is also thought to be a regulatory tonic.

Tea tempers the spirits and harmonizes the mind, dispels lassitude and relieves fatigue, awakens thought and prevents drowsiness, lightens or refreshes the body, and clears the perceptive faculties.

~LuLu, Chinese poet

Teapots & Accoutrements

Just as a woman searches for the perfect purse, the tea lover searches for his favorite teapot. I have many beautiful teapots, antique and new, but my favorite teapots I use on a daily basis have good infusers. I especially like the **Chatsford teapot.** It has an extra-fine, sturdy infuser made to fit perfectly in the teapot that can be used over and over again with a handle (so you don't burn yourself while decaffeinating). The teapots come in clay and bone china. I prefer the bone china because of its durability, and bone china retains the heat longer. My husband and I have our own individual pots we use in the morning since we have very different tastes in tea and share larger teapots with company. The Chatsford infuser also comes in a mug for office use for those wanting to only brew a small amount. I've found that the Chatsford is especially good for brewing very fine infusions such as Rooibos.

The **infuser** is the key to efficient brewing, so you can time how long you brew your tea. Another excellent teapot is the **Swiss Gold Glass** teapot, which can also be put on the burner. The handle doesn't get hot—the filter (23 carat gold-plated metal foil) is neutral to taste. I enjoy a glass teapot for viewing the *agony of the leaves* in larger leaf teas and display teas. Other efficient ways to brew loose tea are the tea sock (cloth) or the t-sak (paper). Part of the discovery of tea is the process and the choices. Many times the Chatsford and the Swiss Gold infusers will fit in some of my antiques teapots. Remember to choose an infuser that does not restrict leaf swelling and circulation of the water. Most tea balls are too small and restrictive for hand-processed, high quality leaves to unfurl fully.

Many hotels put their loose tea in the teapot without an infuser and use a **silver tea strainer** placed over your teacup. It's fun to collect and use the decorative tea strainers, but this method is frustrating because you loose control in how long you brew the tea. I prefer to use a strainer or infuser in the teapot and then remove it after three to five minutes, placing it on a **tea tidy** or small plate. Tea tidies are usually shaped like teapots and have traditionally been used to store your used teabag.

One of the most important elements of enjoying good tea is boiling water (unless you're drinking green tea). Unfortunately boiling water is more difficult to come by in the U.S. if you're eating out, because the coffee machine water is

usually set at 180°. Next to my favorite teapots, I don't think I could live without my **electric water kettle**. There are many on the market. We like the Bodum Curl (47 oz.) for home use and the small Mini Ibis for traveling. The stainless steel Russell Hobbs is also excellent. Most good ones have an automatic shutoff when the water reaches perfect boiling temperature of 212°.

A necessary accoutrement at our home is the **tea cozy**, the coat the teapot wears after brewing to retain heat. Just like clothes, they come in many styles and fabrics. It's fun to collect antique tea cozies as well as new ones. One style my husband calls the "topless, elastic-ruffled sundress tea cozy," fits around the bottom of the teapot. I prefer the hooded kind that covers the whole teapot and fits nice and snug, preferably lined in wool, but you do have to be careful that the handle doesn't get too hot. (My teenage boys used to play around and wear them on their heads.) Cozies extend the length of delicious hot tea for at least 30 minutes. If you don't have a cozy, cover your pot with a dish towel.

One of the favorite customs at my office is to infuse fine quality tea for my friends and share it with them my way. They laugh at my tea cozy, a clean tea shirt sometimes. They love my mugs: crude earthenware that slide onto a tree and have earthy tones. They mostly gawk at the simple Chatsford teapot in blue, and the Russell-Hobbs seems a bit too much—what is the basket and all the fuss about. They all want to come back and have it again. —Bob Sims

Another way to keep your tea warm is using a decorative **tea candle warmer**, made out of many materials—brass, silver, ceramic, glass, etc. This will keep your teapot handle from getting too hot, but may cause your teapot to turn black on the bottom. The fun of all these tea accoutrements is choosing which one you like best.

I'm one of those people who enjoys drinking tea out of a feminine mug or delicate teacup with a sterling-silver spoon. I'm sensitive to touch and color, so I enjoy collecting mugs and teacups that I think will "taste" good, not just look good. I like a handle that I can get my finger into and a cup that's not too heavy to pick up when filled with the beautiful brew. My favorite teaspoons are the English teaspoons or five o'clock American silver teaspoons, larger than a demitasse, but smaller than an average American teaspoon. You can find new ones easily in English department stores or old ones in American antique stores.

Tea Brewing Tricks

Cracked Teapots—Occasionally when brewing tea, especially in a new teapot, "thermal shock" can occur. This is when the teapot or cup cracks because it is heated up too quickly from cold to hot. This has never happened to me personally, but there is no way of knowing if it will happen. Some precautions to take to prevent this are:

1. Heat the teapot with very hot water, but not boiling water before brewing your tea with boiling water.

2. Insert a silver teaspoon in the teapot while pouring the boiling water into the pot. The spoon will absorb the heat before it gets to the teapot.

Brewing Iced Tea—There are many ways to brew iced tea besides handy iced tea machines for home use. Many years ago I used the concentrate method of brewing large tea bags in a glass measuring cup and then pouring hot tea over ice or deluting the tea in a pitcher with cold water. Sometimes I brew loose tea in my large Chatsford teapot (especially finer blends like Rooibos), sweeten with honey if desired while it's hot and then store in a pitcher in the refrigerator. One of the simplest ways to make iced tea is the **cold-overnight method**. Fill up a large t-sak (paper) with loose tea, fastened with a clothespin and immerse in a large pitcher of cold water overnight. The next morning, you'll have delicious iced tea that won't get cloudy. This method also works with other infusions such as Rooibos. Simple syrup or micro-waved honey can be used for sweetening the cold tea. Another trick for brewing large amounts of tea is cutting up clean panty hose as your infuser.

How to Repair Cracked China

When you find a crack in your china, you can mend it with milk. Immerse your cup or dish in a pan with milk to cover. Simmer gently for 45 minutes. Let cool and remove the cup or dish and wash and dry. The protein in the milk is what miraculously repairs the china. Another helpful thing to do when purchasing antique teapots or cups is to ask the vendor if you can fill it with water before you purchase it. Sometimes you can discover fine cracks this way. Another test to determine the condition of the porcelain—using your thumb and index finger, lightly flick your index finger against the teacup. If you hear a high pitched ring, then it's probably fine. If the sound is dull, you may find a chip or a crack.

Tea Etiquette

In the fall of 2002, I had the privilege of attending the American Tea Society Conference in Boulder, Colorado, hosted by Monica Miller and Elizabeth Knight. They offered a wonderful paradox to the attendees that we could be "tea snobs properly"—always make other people comfortable by doing things so well no one really notices the effort. My southern and spiritual roots have always encouraged me that the heart of tea is service—that I create this beautiful, elegant atmosphere with delicious tea treasures, not to impress, but to give. I like Monica Miller's advice, *Use your good manners to make other people feel comfortable, not inferior.*

Since our family of males has experienced a variety of tea gatherings, from elegant affairs to informal, lying-on-the-floor watching the Rose Bowl events, using t-shirts as tea cozies, my list of etiquette rules is quite flexible. The most important thing about teatime is the relational atmosphere. Acceptance and relaxation come before nervousness and fear of making a mistake. Keeping that in mind, here are a few basic etiquette guidelines. For more detailed tea etiquette, I recommend Dorothea Johnson's *Tea & Etiquette.*

Tea can be enjoyed at any time of day—breakfast tea, lunch tea, afternoon tea, evening or dessert tea. What we call it is not important, but for historical reference **"High Tea"** is traditionally served around 6:00 p.m. at a *high table* as a more informal hearty, sit-down meal and sometimes referred to as "meat tea" or supper, serving meat pies, Welsh rarebit, breads, cheese, desserts, and fruits.

Afternoon tea has traditionally been called **"Low Tea,"** served between 3:00 and 5:00 p.m. Afternoon tea has become so popular in the United States, many tearooms extend the teatime from 1:00-6:00 p.m. The title "Low Tea," which I've never actually used, comes from being served at a *low table* (coffee table) with a more delicate menu of scones, finger sandwiches, savories and bite-sized desserts. When champagne or sherry is served, you can refer to it as a **"Royal Tea."**

The kind of tea table you set will be determined by your style—morning English-style cottage-like Brown Betty teapots and mugs or afternoon with formal silver accoutrements and porcelain teacups and saucers. A simpler Asian style with smaller teapots with gaiwans or handleless teacups, a more

contemporary European style with glass teapots—all are appealing. I keep a small tray filled with a sugar bowl of cubed demerera sugar and sugar tongs, creamer, honey dispenser, tea strainer, tea tidy, container for artificial sweetener, and a spooner filled with my favorite teaspoons, always ready to bring out for tea time. A last minute teatime is not a hassle—just choose a pot, some tea, teacups, and turn on the kettle.

Flatware—for a seated tea, there should be at each place a knife or small spreader on the right side of the plate, a dessert or curd fork on the left side. The teaspoon may be placed on the saucer holding the teacup or to the right of the knife. It's definitely improper to use one's own utensils to dip into jam or cream dishes.

Serving the Tea—The host or hostess always pours the first cup of tea (three-quarters full) and is aware when the kettle needs to be turned on again for a second pot. Pouring almost to the rim of the cup is a faux pas.

Napkins—Napkins were originally towel size and used for doggie bags. Today it's proper to take the napkin off the table before unfolding it on your lap. Luncheon and tea napkins can be unfolded fully; dinner napkins are folded in half with the fold against your waist. Blot your mouth with the napkin, don't wipe, and if you need to leave the table, place your napkin on your chair.

Holding the cups—Place your index finger through the handle with your thumb just above it for support and the second finger below the handle for added security, keeping your pinkie finger hidden. The extended pinkie is a faux pas today along with cradling the cup in one's fingers when it has a handle. If you're enjoying tea while standing or seated more than 12 inches from a table, be sure to lift the saucer along with your teacup holding it with one hand while you sip from the teacup with your other hand.

Stirring the tea—Stirring a cup of tea is done gently and quietly back and forth with a teaspoon in the center of the cup, then placing the teaspoon on the saucer behind the cup with the handle pointing in the same direction as the teacup handle at four o'clock. Swirling the tea as if it were a wine glass is a faux pas. (On a cruise ship, we noticed the waiter's signal for serving tea instead of coffee to a guest was leaving the spoon upright in an empty teacup.)

Scones—There are several ways to eat scones; the size of the scone may determine your choice. The same etiquette for eating bread applies. Always spoon your clotted cream, lemon curd, or jam onto your plate, never directly onto the scone. Slice the scone horizontally with a knife. Then either spread one bite at a time with jam before eating or spread jam only on the bottom half and pick up that half and eat before spreading the top half. One big faux pas is putting the scone halves back together after preparing them with the jam and cream and eating like a sandwich. However, you may eat your scone with a knife and fork American or continental style. If the scone is very small I think it proper to apply jam to the top and eat without dividing in half.

Tea bags—We don't usually prefer tea bags, but it's nice to know the etiquette involved since most restaurants use them. The preferred service is to request a saucer to put the used teabag on instead of placing it on your teacup saucer where you'll end up with a dripping teacup. A big faux pas is draining a tea bag by winding the string around a spoon. Another one which we all do is picking up the tea bag by the tab and jiggling it up and down in the water to hasten the brewing time.

Milk and Sugar—Many used to put milk in their teacup first to prevent cracking the fine porcelain and reducing tea stains, but according to modern-day etiquette experts, it's proper to put the tea in first and then the milk. Sugar cubes are preferred for their neatness and the ritual of using elegant sugar tongs.

> *The soul of politeness is not a question of rules but of*
> *tranquillity, humility, and simplicity. And in the taking of tea*
> *it finds perhaps its most perfect expression.*
>
> —*Tea & Etiquette*, Dorothea Johnson

The Tea Menu

Tea times can be very simple from a few sweet treats or a cream scone to a very elaborate menu with four or five courses. In England, the traditional afternoon tea includes scones and tea sandwiches along with sweets. In France, afternoon tea is usually a pot of tea and a dessert. My favorite menu for afternoon tea usually includes:

Tea sandwiches (meat and vegetarian)
Savories (egg and cheese)

Scones (with lemon curd, clotted cream, and/or preserves)

Fruit

A Chocolate confection

A fruit-flavored or nut-flavored confection (preferably lemon or almond)

Cake (optional)

The following recipes are some of my favorites for tea time. There are many delicious tea companions in other sections of the cookbook. The Cheese Wafers (page 32) and Carol's Quiche (page 40) are excellent savories. Other sweets include: Ryan's Lemon Iced Bars (page 111), Death by Chocolate Cookies (page 99), Hanau Chocolate Mint Squares (page 105), Caramel Slice (page 109), Spritz Cookies (page 102), Cranberry Caramel Bars (page 103), Cream Cheese Pound Cake (page 122), and Strawberries on a Cloud (page 113).

In the United States, we freely borrow from many different cultures to our advantage. We can be the entrepreneurs of "afternoon tea," crafting our own menus and establishing new traditions, intertwining the old with the new. Our tearoom dreams can be experienced in our own homes with family and friends. What an exciting adventure to be a part of the tea movement sweeping our nation in the new millennium. Enjoy these recipes and create some of your own—treasures to discover that will last a lifetime—not only the edible ones but also the conversations, contemplations, and relations that are a part of the magic of tea time.

When we sit and have our tea, we are transported back to your wonderful inn, with its warmth and caring. We find we leave our work behind and talk of our future together, have wonderful fantasies and make wonderful plans. All too soon, our teatime is over, yet the feelings linger, allowing us to be in a more gentle and acceptable place...

Carol & Malcolm Cohen, Brooklyn, NY
(Tea-Time at the Inn by Gail Greco)

Tea Time Recipes

Tea Sandwiches

English Sandwich Loaf

1 loaf fresh unsliced white bread
1 loaf fresh unsliced whole wheat
   or dark bread
   Soft butter

3 Fillings: ham salad, pimento
   cheese, chicken salad, egg salad,
   or cucumber and cream cheese
12 ounces cream cheese
   Heavy whipping cream
   Electric Knife

Ham salad: An easy way to make this is to get thinly sliced deli ham (Boar's Head Black Forrest) ¼ pound for one loaf.

Take all the sliced ham in a stack and slice it into tiny pieces. In a bowl, add 2 tablespoons sweet pickle relish and 2 tablespoons mayonnaise and mix. This can also be made in a food processor.

Pimento Cheese: 4 ounces grated sharp Cheddar cheese and Monterey Jack cheese, 10 ounces red pimentos, drained, 2 tablespoons mayonnaise, fresh dill. (Central Market has wonderful pimento cheese in their deli section.)

Egg Salad: 4 hard-boiled eggs (boil for 15 minutes), seasoned salad salt and pepper, 3 tablespoons mayonnaise. Mash eggs with a fork. Add mayonnaise and seasonings or mix in food processor.

Chicken Salad: 1½ cups cooked, cubed chicken breast, ¼ cup chopped celery (tiny pieces), 1 green onion sliced very thinly (whole onion), 1 tablespoon capers, ¼ teaspoon curry, salt salad seasoning. (Culpepper's from England is excellent.) ¼ cup mayonnaise plus 1 tablespoon sour cream—can add a little fresh cilantro. Blend together and let sit in the refrigerator several hours before using.

Cucumbers & cream cheese: Slice cucumbers very thinly, may use plain cream cheese or vegi cream cheese, salt salad seasoning. Mix together with fresh watercress.

Cream Cheese Icing: In KitchenAid, mix 12 ounces cream cheese with small amount of whipping cream until it reaches a nice consistency for icing the loaf.

The best way to prepare the unsliced bread is with an electric knife. Slice each loaf lengthwise into equal ½ to ¾-inch slices. Arrange the horizontal slices on top of each other alternating white with wheat bread using 4 slices per loaf. Using the electric knife, decrust the bread as it is stacked like a cake, so the layers are even with each other. Spread 3 slices with butter, leaving the top slice plain. Spread the bottom layer with the ham or chicken salad. Place next slice on top. On second layer spread pimento cheese. On third slice spread egg salad or cream cheese with sliced cucumbers with seasoning—can add watercress or sunflower sprouts to this layer. After placing top slice of bread, ice the loaf with cream cheese icing (thin layer). After covering the loaf, you can add decoration with the icing in a pastry bag and garnishes to the top (red pepper, olives, etc.) Keep in the refrigerator until use. Slice with electric knife ¾ to 1-inch slices (8 to 10 per loaf). The nice thing about this loaf, you don't have to worry about it drying out if you use fresh bread.

Cucumber Sandwiches

White bread	Softened butter
Round or heart-shaped cookie cutter	Cream cheese with favorite seasoning
Cucumber	

Using cookie cutters, cut out bread slices. Spread butter on bread, then cream cheese mixture. Slice cucumber into round, paper thin slices (or use tiny heart-shaped cookie cutters) and place on top of each piece of bread. (You can marinate the cucumber slices in the Celery Seed Dressing.) Sprinkle with pepper, paprika, or parsley. Store in airtight container with damp paper towel under and on top of sandwiches.

Taylor's Curry Chicken Salad Tea Sandwiches

4   cups cooked, cubed chicken
     breasts
1   cup sliced red seedless grapes
1   cup chopped apples
1   cup roasted sliced almonds

1   tablespoon roasted curry powder
     (roast in nonstick pan for few
     minutes)
1   cup mayonnaise
⅓   cup nonfat yogurt

Mix all ingredients and store in the refrigerator until needed for tea sandwiches.

Charyl Coleman and Margery Taylor

Salmon Tea Sandwiches

Gilled or smoked salmon
   (I prefer grilled salmon which
   I will do the night before.
   I grill a very large salmon for
   dinner and save leftover for
   tea sandwiches.)

Soft cream cheese
Jalapeño jelly
Red bell peppers, sliced into
   small pieces
Pumpernickel bread or lahvosh
   crackers

Spread cream cheese on buttered bread or on each lahvosh cracker. Add small amount of jelly followed by sliced salmon. The sandwiches can be made ahead of time and kept in Tupperware with dampened paper towels. The lahvosh crackers need to be made right before your party begins.

Chicken and Cranberry Sandwiches

2   chicken breasts, finely chopped
6   ounces cream cheese, softened
½   cup dried cranberries

1   teaspoon grated orange peel
    Thinly sliced white bread

Fold together all the above ingredients and spread on bread making sandwiches. Remove the crusts and cut into desired shapes.

Date Bacon Sandwiches

4 ounces cream cheese
⅓ cup pitted dates, finely chopped

5 slices bacon, cooked crisp and crumbled
12 slices pumpernickel bread

Beat cream cheese until light; mix in dates and bacon. Spread mixture on 6 of the bread slices, top with remaining slices. Remove crusts and quarter each sandwich diagonally.

Scones

Carol's Cream Scones

2 cups sifted flour
2 teaspoons baking powder
4 tablespoons sugar
6 tablespoons cold unsalted butter

¼ cup dried cranberries (soaked in 2 tablespoons Taylors Cream Sherry)
½-¾ cup heavy cream

Sift flour with baking powder and sugar. In KitchenAid mixer, cut in cold butter until crumbly. Add cranberries and sherry. Mix, slowly adding the cream until dough forms a ball and comes off the edge of the mixer. You can roll the dough out with flour or you can do it the Martha Stewart way by putting on your surface a large piece of Saran Wrap. Put a ball of your dough on top of wrap. Place another large piece of Saran Wrap over ball. Roll out carefully with rolling pin on top of wrap, so dough is ½ to ¾-inch thick for small scones and ¾ to 1-inch thick for larger ones. Cut scones with biscuit cutter and place on a lightly greased pan. (I use Silpat baking sheets.) Brush each scone with heavy cream before baking at 425° for 10 to 12 minutes.

Carol Sims

If you want to omit the cranberries and add another dried fruit or lemon zest, feel free, remember to keep the Sherry in the recipe for that extra something special.

Orange Current Scones

3 cups flour	12 tablespoons unsalted butter (1½ sticks)
⅓ cup sugar	¾ cup currents (soaked in brandy)
2½ teaspoons baking powder	1-2 teaspoons grated orange peel
½ teaspoon baking soda	1 cup buttermilk
¾ teaspoon salt	

Mix dry ingredients. Cut in butter. Stir in currents and orange peel. Add buttermilk. Stir until just moisten. Roll out, cut with cookie cutter. Bake on greased sheet at 425° for 12 minutes.

Pumpkin Scones

3 cups sifted self-rising flour	1 teaspoon cinnamon
½ cup sugar	¼ cup raisins or dried cranberries
½ cup unsalted butter	⅓ cup canned pumpkin
¼ teaspoon freshly grated nutmeg	¼ cup heavy cream

Cut the butter into the flour and sugar with a KitchenAid mixer until coarse. Add spices and raisins or cranberries. Slowly mix in pumpkin, then cream until dough forms a ball in the mixer. Roll dough on floured surface or between two pieces of plastic wrap ½-inch thick. Cut out scones with biscuit cutter. Place on greased baking sheet or on silpat sheets. Brush with heavy cream before baking at 400° for 10 to 12 minutes until lightly brown. Enjoy with clotted cream or add frosting of milk, confectioners' sugar and a little canned pumpkin.

There are few hours in life more aggreeable than
the hour dedicated to the ceremony known as afternoon tea.

~Henry James

Crispy Scones

2	cups sifted flour		¾	teaspoon salt
½	cup sugar		½	cup chilled unsalted butter
2	teaspoons cream of tartar		½	cup dates
1	teaspoon baking soda		2	eggs slightly beaten

In a large bowl, sift flour, add dry ingredients, then sift again. Cut the butter into small cubes. Using a pastry cutter, blend the butter with the flour mixture until it resembles coarse crumbs. Add dates. Mix egg mixture in until dough forms a ball. Roll out on lightly floured surface or between Saran Wrap, cut with cookie cutters. Brush with beaten egg. Bake on greased pan, 400° for 15 minutes.

Lori Martino

Delight your guests with homemade lemon curd and clotted cream when serving scones. It's quite easy and stores in the refrigerator.

Lemon Curd

⅔	cup fresh lemon juice (4 to 5 lemons)		4	large or 5 medium eggs (blended thoroughly in blender)
	Grated rind from 2 lemons		3	tablespoons butter
½	cup plus 2 tablespoons sugar			

Place juice, rind, and sugar into the top of a double boiler over boiling water. Stir until the sugar has dissolved, then stir in the beaten eggs. Add 1 tablespoon butter and stir until melted. Repeat until all the butter has been added. Continue cooking and stirring until the curd has the consistency of thick cream. Pour into jars and refrigerate. Eat within 4 weeks.

Carol Sims

Delicious served on scones with American clotted cream or Devonshire cream.

American Clotted Cream

2 (8-ounce) packages cream cheese, softened	½ cup whipping cream
	1 teaspoon vanilla
¼ cup sugar	

Whip all ingredients in KitchenAid until creamy and smooth. Store in covered container in refrigerator using the dates on the cream cheese and whipping cream.

Try English Clotted Cream by The Devon Cream Company (pasteurized in dairy)—the real thing.

Devonshire Cream

½ cup whipping cream	¼ cup sour cream

Whip cream until stiff. Fold in sour cream and chill until ready to serve. Split a scone across the middle, then top with jam or Lemon Curd and add Devonshire Cream. This can also be sweetened with powdered sugar or liqueur and served with fruit.

Welsh Cakes

A favorite of Jonathan & mine for tea time.

2 cups self-rising flour	⅔ cup sugar
Pinch of salt	⅔ cup dried currants
¼ cup vegetable shortening	1 egg, beaten
¼ cup butter, chilled	1 tablespoon milk

Sift flour and salt. Cut in shortening and butter until mixture resembles bread crumbs. Stir in sugar and currants. Add egg and a little milk, if necessary, to make soft, but not sticky dough. On a floured surface, roll out dough to ¼-inch thick. Cut out circles. Cook cakes on a hot griddle over low heat until golden brown (about 3 minutes). Dust with powdered sugar.

Carol Sims

Tea Time Recipes

Sweet Tea Treats

Shortbread Cookies

4 sticks butter (1 pound)	1 cup sugar (very fine)
4-5 cups flour	

Cream butter and sugar a long time. Add flour and beat for 5 minutes. Roll out dough ¼-inch thick and cut with cookie cutter. Bake on ungreased cookie sheet 300° for 20 to 30 minutes until slightly golden brown. Keeps well in freezer.

Carol Sims

These are very special cut out of a heart-shaped cookie cutter.

Orange Macaroons

1 pound almond paste (2 packages)	Zest of 1 orange
½ cup powdered sugar plus more for rolling	2 large egg whites
	⅛ teaspoon pure almond extract

Heat oven to 350°. Line 2 baking sheets with silpats. Mix in bowl of an electric mixer almond paste and sugar. Beat until creamy, about 2 minutes. Add orange zest and beat to combine. Add 1 egg white and almond extract and mix 1 minute more.

On a lightly sugared surface, roll into two ¾-inch-wide logs, about 18 inches long. Cut each log crosswise into thirty pieces about ½ inch wide each. Roll into balls. Lightly beat remaining egg white. Coat each ball with egg white, and roll in sugar, tapping to remove excess. Place on prepared baking sheets, about 30 per sheet. Let rest for 30 minutes. Pinch with three fingers to form an irregular pyramid shape. Bake until lightly golden, about 15 minutes. Transfer to wire rack and cool completely. Can freeze.

Macaroon Kisses

⅓	cup softened butter	1¼	cups flour
1	(4-ounce) package cream cheese	2	teaspoons baking powder
¾	cup sugar	¼	teaspoon salt
1	egg yolk	5	cups sweetened coconut flakes
2	teaspoons almond extract	1	bag Hershey's Chocolate Kisses
2	teaspoons orange juice		

Beat butter, cream cheese, and sugar until well blended. Add egg yolk, almond extract, and orange juice, beating well. Stir together flour, baking powder, and salt; gradually add to butter mixture, beating until well blended. Stir in 3 cups of coconut flakes. Cover and refrigerate for 1 hour until firm enough to handle. Heat oven to 350°. Shape dough into 1-inch balls; roll balls into remaining coconut. Place on ungreased cookie sheet. Bake 10 to 12 minutes or until lightly browned. After removing from oven, immediately place unwrapped Hershey kisses on top of each cookie. Cool.

Makes about 4 dozen cookies

Almond Meringue Cookies

Inspired by my tea trip to Paris.

3	egg whites	1	teaspoon Almond Extract
1	cup sugar	¾	cup sliced almonds
¼	teaspoon cream of tartar		

Heat oven to 400°. Beat egg whites until a little fluffy in an electric mixer. Add cream of tartar and begin beating on high until stiff. Gradually add sugar until the egg white mixture is thick and glassy. Beat in the almond extract and fold in by hand the almonds. Drop onto a cookie sheet lined with parchment paper. Before putting in the oven, turn off the oven completely. You may leave these in the oven overnight. The cookies may be eaten when the oven is completely cool, several hours.

Carol Sims

The most fun part of making these cookies is licking the batter.

Potato Chip Cookies

½ pound butter (2 sticks)
½ cup sugar
1   teaspoon vanilla

1½ cups flour
¾   cup crushed potato chips

Cream butter and sugar. Add rest of ingredients. Bake at 350° for 15 to 20 minutes.

Carol Sims

Charleston Cream Cheese Cookies

1   stick butter
1   stick margarine
1   (8-ounce) package cream cheese
2   cups sugar

2   cups flour
2   teaspoons vanilla
½   cup pecans, chopped

Cream together butter and margarine. Add rest of ingredients, beating after each. Stir in nuts. Drop by half teaspoon on greased cookie sheet. Bake at 350° until edges are brown, about 15 minutes. Watch carefully, burn easily.

Carol Sims

Sesame Seed Cookies

½ cup sesame seeds
1   tablespoon butter
1   cup brown sugar
3   tablespoons flour

1   egg beaten
1   teaspoon vanilla
¼   teaspoon salt

Mix together. Dust pan with flour. Brown sesame seeds slightly before using. Bake 350° for 5 to 8 minutes.

Ann Eidschun Shotmeyer

Sand Tarts

A favorite of my boys.

1	cup butter	2	cups flour
1	teaspoon vanilla	1	cup ground nuts
¼	cup powdered sugar		

Cream butter, adding vanilla. Add sugar, cream well. Add flour and nuts (pecans), mix well. Divide dough in pieces the size of walnuts, shape into crescents. Bake on unoiled sheet for 40 minutes at 300° degrees. Roll in powdered sugar while warm. Freezes well.

Lime Meltaways

¾	cup (1½ sticks) unsalted butter at room temperature	1	tablespoon pure vanilla extract
1	cup powdered sugar	1¾	cups flour
	Grated zest of two limes	2	tablespoons cornstarch
2	tablespoons freshly squeezed lime juice	¼	teaspoon salt

Cream butter with electric mixer and ⅓ cup sugar until fluffy. Add lime zest, lime juice, and vanilla extract and beat until fluffy.

In another bowl, whisk together flour, cornstarch, and salt. Add flour mixture to butter mixture and beat on low speed.

Between 2 (8 x 12-inch) pieces of parchment paper, roll dough into 2 (1¼-inch) diameter logs. Chill until firm, at least 1 hour.

Heat oven to 350°. Line baking sheets with silpats (nonstick liners). Remove parchment paper from logs. Slice ⅓-inch slices on pan. Bake until barely golden for 12 to 15 minutes. Cool on wire rack for 5 minutes. Then while still warm, place cookies in plastic bag filled with the rest of the powdered sugar and coat. Store cookies in airtight container. You can store uncooked dough in freezer. This is a great cookie for tea time.

Lemon Posset

3¾ cups whipping cream
1   cup plus 2 tablespoons sugar

Juice of 4 large lemons
(½ to ¾ cup)

Combine cream and sugar in a saucepan. Bring to a boil. Simmer 2 to 3 minutes. Stir in lemon juice. Cool slightly. Pour into small stemware glasses. Refrigerate for 2 hours or more. Decorate with whipped cream, a lemon slice, and a raspberry and serve with shortbread.

Linda Leamer's (teatimegazette.com)—Commodore Hotel, Instow, North Devon

Possets were popular in medieval times and made of hot milk or cream curdled with ale or wine. They were often sweetened and spiced, and some had eggs and butter added. These semi-solid drinks were supped from a bowl and used to revive people who had been chilled from traveling. The above recipe can be served for the fruit entrée during afternoon tea.

Tut's Toffee

35 saltine crackers
2   sticks butter
1   cup brown sugar

1   (12-ounce) package semi-sweet
    chocolate chips
1   cup pecans, chopped

Preheat oven to 350°. Line 10 x 15-inch jelly-roll pan with aluminum foil. Place saltines (7 down, 5 across) in pan. Combine brown sugar and butter in glass bowl and microwave on high for 4 minutes. Stir thoroughly and pour over crackers. Bake at 350° for 20 minutes. Remove from oven and cover with chocolate chips. When chips melt, smooth over with spatula. Sprinkle with chopped nuts. Chill for ½ hour in freezer. Break into bite-sized pieces.

Carol Sims

Treat from Two Meeting Street Inn in Charleston. This treat is just the right amount of chocolate for afternoon tea time.

Hors d'oeuvres & Beverages

Spinach/Basil Cheese Ball

Yummy and very easy. Everyone likes this!

1   (8-ounce) package cream cheese
1   (4-ounce) goat cheese
1   cup fresh baby spinach leaves
1   cup fresh basil
¼   cup olive oil
½   cup Parmesan cheese

2   cloves of garlic
    Pepper to taste
½   cup pine nuts
½   cup dried cranberries or sun-
    dried tomatoes

Mix in small food processor spinach leaves, basil, garlic, and olive oil. Mix until smooth. Add Parmesan cheese. Mix cream cheese and goat cheese with mixer until smooth. Line a small 5-inch bowl with Saran Wrap. Spray inside with pan. Line inside of the bowl with a layer of ½ of cream cheese mixture. Then add all of basil mixture, all of the pine nuts, dried cranberries, and the remainder of the cream cheese. Cover with plastic wrap and refrigerate for at least 30 minutes. Several hours is best. Serve upside down on a plate with lahvosh crackers.

Kimberly Timmins—with a few changes from Carol

Artichoke Dip

2   (14-ounce) cans artichoke,
    drained and chopped
1   cup mayonnaise
1   cup Parmesan cheese

¼   teaspoon season salt
    Dash cayenne pepper
¼-½ teaspoon garlic salt

Mix together and bake in casserole dish at 350° for 25 to 30 minutes. Serve with Triscuits.

Pat Chapman

Nine Layer Dip

*I've eaten this dip in many homes but couldn't
find it in any of my recipe books, so I had to include it.*

1	(15-ounce) can refried beans with jalapeños	2	cups grated cheese (Cheddar or Mexican mix)
1	cup sour cream	1	cup shredded lettuce (already prepared shredded lettuce in a bag)
1	cup guacamole (fresh or already prepared from produce department—Classic)	2	large tomatoes chopped
1	pound cooked hamburger meat prepared with Lowry's Taco Mix	1	can sliced black olives
		2	green onion tops sliced

Layer the ingredients in order listed in a 9 x 13-inch glass dish. Refrigerate for several hours before serving with your favorite corn tortilla chips.

Mary Durham

Cheese Wafers

2	sticks butter	1	teaspoon cayenne pepper
½	pound sharp cheese, grated	1	teaspoon salt
2	cups flour		

Cream butter with electric mixer. Add grated cheese, flour, salt, and pepper. Shape into 1½-inch log roll in wax paper. Chill in the refrigerator overnight. Preheat oven 325°. Slice thin round pieces and place one half pecan on each slice. Bake for 15 to 25 minutes or until done. Cool before serving. May be stored in freezer.

I think these taste best a little crispy, so be sure to cook them long enough.

Ann Burney Eidschun Shotmeyer (my mother)

Spinach Dip

Like Houstons in Atlanta

2 packages Stouffers Creamed Spinach (thawed)
1 (14-ounce) jar artichoke hearts, drained and chopped
4 ounces Monterey Jack cheese, grated

2 ounces Monterey Jack cheese with jalapeños grated
¾ cup Parmesan cheese grated
Splash of Tabasco
¼ teaspoon garlic powder

Combine ingredients in a bowl. Put in lightly greased dish. Bake at 350° for about 20 minutes. Serve with sour cream, salsa and tostadas.

Helen Maddox (my first cousin from Atlanta, Georgia)

Sims Salsa

10 fresh Romano tomatoes
1 red onion
1 ounce fresh cilantro

4-6 serrano peppers (depending on how hot you want it)
Garlic salt
1 lime

1. Coarsely chop tomatoes and ⅔ of the onion. Chop cilantro or use an herb grinder. Grind serrano peppers in an herb grinder, or chop finely with knife; the finer the serrano, the better the flavor. Combine in food processor and blend, leaving small chunks of tomatoes and onions.

2. Stir in about 2 teaspoons garlic salt, or to taste. Squeeze ¼ of a lime and stir. Serve with El Lago tortilla chips and enjoy.

Tips: the finer you chop the peppers, the hotter they get. The more onion you add to the peppers, the hotter the salsa will be in combination with the peppers. You can never go wrong with too much garlic salt.

Jonathan Sims

Dill Snack Crackers

1	box oyster crackers	½	cup canola or olive oil
2	tablespoons dill weed	1	package dry ranch dressing

In a large zip lock bag, dump crackers. In a small bowl, mix other ingredients and then pour mixture into the zip lock bag over the crackers. Shake and let sit overnight. Store in an airtight container.

Julia Brown (Bob's Aunt Julia from Guntersville, Alabama)

Savannah Rooibos Tea Punch

Brew 6 cups Savannah Rooibos (Rooibos with cocoa pieces, almond bits, and chocolate-rum flavoring) for 5 minutes the day before you want to use it or 4 hours before the party. Add two tablespoons of sugar or 3 tablespoons of honey to the tea while hot. Pour into ice cubes or a mold; freeze that and refrigerate the rest of the tea. You may need to make more tea depending on how much punch you need. About 30 minutes before you're ready for the punch, whip 1 cup of whipping cream in an electric mixer and add 1 teaspoon of vanilla extract and 2 tablespoons of powdered sugar to the whipped cream. Fold the whipped cream into the cold tea, add the tea ice cubes or frozen mold and serve out of a decorative pitcher or punch bowl. Sprinkle with fresh nutmeg. The Savannah Rooibos is also delicious hot. When you add milk or cream to many of these Rooibos blends, it feels like someone has wrapped a cozy blanket around you, very comforting.

Carol Sims

*One cup enjoyed, one refreshing sip and all the differences of opinion,
even hostility cease. A headache vanishes. Courage returns.*

~**Author unknown**

Peach or Oasis Rooibos Iced Tea

Brew 3 overflowing tablespoons of peach or oasis Rooibos tea in a 6-cup Chatsford teapot with the infuser with boiling water for 5 to 10 minutes. Take out the infuser and stir in 4 tablespoons of wildflower honey into hot tea and stir until the honey is melted. Pour tea into pitcher and store in the refrigerator. Serve when cold over ice with fresh lemon.

This is a very healthy drink for children and adults with lots of potassium and other minerals and no caffeine.

Carol Sims

Fruit Smoothies

*We've been making fruit smoothies at our home for over 30 years, before they were popular. My favorite is during the peach season. This recipe actually came from visiting Italy in 1969. The bartenders all had big bowls of fresh peaches on their bars and made an alcoholic drink called a **Roger**. When I returned to the states, I copied that recipe without liquor. This is what I came up with along with some variations:*

Mix in the blender:
1	cup apple juice		Juice of 1 lemon
2	fresh peaches, peeled and sliced (can be frozen)	2	cups ice

You can add a little sugar if it's not sweet enough and other fruit such as bananas, strawberries, and mangoes.

Original Roger *recipe mixed in blender:*
2	jiggers of vodka		Juice of 1 lemon
2	big fresh peaches, peeled and sliced	2	tablespoons sugar
		2	cups ice

Tea Smoothy

In a blender, mix 1 cup of your favorite unsweetened iced tea, fresh cut-up fruit such as peaches, mangoes, or strawberries, juice of one lemon or ¼ cup of orange juice, 2 tablespoons of sugar or honey, lots of ice. Mix in the blender until thick and smooth. Yummy and healthy.

Carol Sims

Margaritas

1   (4-ounce) can frozen Minute Maid limeade

Empty frozen limeade into the blender. Fill ⅓ can with Cointreau and pour into blender. Fill ¾ can with Tequila. Fill blender ¾ full of ice and blend until smooth and thick.

Yummy Plaza Punch

1   quart fresh orange juice
1   pint fresh lime juice
1   pint fresh lemon juice
1   pint can pineapple juice
1   pint can pink grapefruit juice

2   pint strawberries blended with some of juice in blender
½   cup grenadine
½   cup coconut milk

Mix above ingredients in blender and add 1 liter of ginger ale.

Carol Sims—the bartender at the Plaza Club in San Antonio shared his secret nonalcoholic punch with me.

Wedding Punch

1	(12-ounce) can orange juice	6	cups water
1	(12-ounce) can lemonade	1	(46-ounce) can pineapple juice
4	cups sugar	5	bananas-mixed in blender

Mix and freeze in pints. Mix 1 pint frozen mixture to 1 bottle ginger ale.

Jim's Orange Jewel

¼	cup Tang	1	cup water
½	cup milk	2	tablespoons sugar
½	teaspoon vanilla	2	cups crushed ice

Mix the first 5 ingredients together in blender, then add ice.

Jim Sims

Eggnog

6	eggs, separated	1	pint milk
1	cup sugar	1½	cups liquor, rum, or 1 teaspoon
1	pint whipping cream or vanilla		vanilla extract
	ice cream softened		Grated nutmeg (fresh)

Beat egg whites until fluffy, gradually beat in ½ cup sugar.

Beat egg yolks until pale yellow and fluffy, gradually beat in remaining sugar. Fold whites into yolks. Add cream, milk, and liquors or vanilla. Serve sprinkled with nutmeg.

The quick way to make eggnog is to buy Borden's or Promiseland Eggnog and add 1 pint of Haagen Dazs vanilla ice cream and 1 cup of whipped heavy cream, sprinkled with fresh nutmeg.

Carol Sims—delicious!

Breakfast & Breads

Good Company Eggs

½ pound grated Swiss or
   mozzarella cheese
4 tablespoons butter
1 cup heavy cream
½ teaspoon salt

Dash pepper
1½ teaspoons dry mustard
   (or 1 teaspoon fresh mustard)
12 eggs
4 ounces cream cheese

Grease glass rectangular baking dish. Spread grated cheese on bottom of dish. Dot with butter. Then dot with cut-up cream cheese spread evenly over dish. Mix cream with seasonings. Pour half of cream over cheese. Add eggs (beaten in blender). Pour rest of cream on top. Bake at 325° for 45 to 50 minutes or until puffed up and center is done-looks a little like a soufflé. Garnish with parsley and serve with sausage or bacon.

Carol Sims

This original recipe was enjoyed by my husband and I while visiting the Charleston House Bed & Breakfast in Woodstock, Vermont. I've added the cream cheese. Cream cheese is the secret ingredient to any egg dish, especially quiches!

Muffin Pan Eggs

6 eggs (or as many as you desire)
1 cup grated Cheddar cheese
6 pieces of slightly cooked bacon
   (microwave does the trick)

Pinch salt
Dash pepper

Spray generously a muffin pan with vegetable cooking spray. In the bottom of each muffin pan, place one bacon strip broken in half and crisscrossed. Then break a fresh egg into each muffin slot on top of the bacon. Sprinkle each egg with grated cheese and salt and pepper. Bake at 350° for 20 minutes or until eggs are cooked as you like them.

Marian Thompson

This is an easy recipe for lots of people. Most people can eat at least two egg muffins.

Sausage Egg Casserole

Remember you need to make this the night before!

6	slices white or whole wheat bread	6	eggs
8	ounces of whipped cream cheese	1	teaspoons dry mustard (or 1 teaspoon fresh mustard)
1	pound ground sausage	1	teaspoon salt
4	cups shredded Cheddar or mixed Mexican cheese	1	teaspoon pepper
		2	cups half-and-half

Lightly butter each slice of bread, then spread with softened cream cheese. Place bread in a 9 x 13-inch buttered glass baking dish. Brown sausage and drain. Sprinkle sausage over bread and sprinkle cheese over sausage. Blend eggs and half-and-half in the blender, adding spices. Pour egg mixture over bread, sausage, and cheese. Cover with foil and refrigerate overnight. At this point, it may be frozen until ready to use. Remove from freezer and thaw overnight in the refrigerator. Bake 50 to 60 minutes at 350° until casserole is puffed up, bubbly and lightly brown on top. Let sit for 5 to 10 minutes before serving.

You can add chopped green chilies or jalapeños as well as onions to the sausage while browning for a spicier dish.

Carol Sims

Cottage Cheese Pancakes

4	eggs	2	tablespoons canola oil
1	cup cottage cheese	½	cup sifted flour
¼	teaspoon salt		

Mix all ingredients in blender and blend on low speed until cheese curds disappear. Drop by tablespoons onto hot nonstick skillet. Best if not made too big. Serve immediately when hot with favorite topping.

These pancakes were a favorite at our home. My favorite topping is pure maple syrup heated in the microwave or fresh or frozen blueberries that have been heated in the microwave until they pop and create their own juice.

Carol's Quiche

My boys love this recipe!

1 prepared uncooked pie shell (made fresh or I use the Pillsbury refrigerated pie shell in the red package)	4 eggs
	1 teaspoon dry mustard (or 1 teaspoon fresh mustard)
	1 teaspoon salt
1 cup fresh baby spinach	½ teaspoon pepper
4 pieces of cooked bacon crumbled	1 cup half & half or heavy cream
4 ounces softened cream cheese	1-2 cups mozzarella cheese

Prepare pastry shell in glass or ceramic pie dish. Spread cream cheese on the bottom only of the unbaked pie shell. Layer fresh spinach leaves, bacon, and grated cheese. Mix eggs, cream, and seasonings in the blender. Pour over shell so most of ingredients are covered. If your pie shell is larger than normal, you may add another egg to the blended mixture. Bake in 350° oven until done for 35 to 50 minutes. The egg mixture should puff up when done. Shake the pie gently to see if the middle is done. Let sit 5 to 10 minutes before serving.

Carol Sims

You can also make this in small pastry shells for individual servings with shorter baking time.

New England Pancakes

2 large eggs, lightly beaten	Pinch freshly grated nutmeg
½ cup flour, sifted	1 tablespoon unsalted butter
½ cup milk	Confectioners' sugar for dusting
Pinch salt	

Heat oven to 425°. Whisk together eggs, flour, milk, salt, and nutmeg until well combined or mix in blender. This batter can be made a day ahead and kept in the refrigerator. Melt butter in a 12-inch cast-iron skillet over medium heat. Pour batter into pan and transfer to oven. Bake until pancake is golden brown and puffy, 10 to 12 minutes. Transfer to serving plate and dust with confectioners' sugar and serve with fresh fruit or maple syrup.

Swedish Pancakes

¾ cup flour	4 tablespoons butter, melted
1½ cups milk	(divided into 1 and 3)
3 eggs	2 teaspoons sugar
	⅛ teaspoon salt

In medium bowl or blender (I choose blender), mix together flour and ¼ cup milk. Add eggs, remaining milk, 3 tablespoons melted butter, sugar, and salt. Beat until batter is smooth. Heat a small skillet and brush some of the remaining butter in skillet. Pour 2 to 3 tablespoons batter into hot pan. Tilt the pan so the batter evenly covers the entire surface in a thin layer. Cook 2 to 3 minutes or until the underside is golden. With a spatula, carefully turn the pancake over and continue cooking until light browned. Remove pancake to plate. Fill the inside of pancake with lemon curd or heated blackberry or raspberry jelly and roll up. Sprinkle with powdered sugar and serve with a dollop of sour cream.

Carol Sims

Light as a Cloud Pancakes

6 egg yolks	1 teaspoon salt
2 cups cottage cheese	¼ teaspoon nutmeg
⅔ cup flour	Pinch cream of tartar
2 tablespoons sugar	

Beat 6 egg whites with a pinch of cream of tartar until stiff, but not dry. Mix all other ingredients in the blender until smooth. Fold the egg whites into blended mixture. Heat skillet on low. Use about ¼ cup batter per pancake on greased skillet (if needed). These pancakes may not bubble to tell you when they are done, so watch carefully. A light, but dense treat served with fresh maple syrup.

Carol Sims

Jonathan's Pancakes

1	cup flour	4	tablespoons brown sugar
2	teaspoons baking powder	1	large egg
½	teaspoons salt	1	cup milk
2	tablespoons butter, melted plus some for the griddle		

Mix together and you've got a delicious pancake batter.

Yummy recipe from my son Jonathan Sims.

Cinnamon Bread Custard

Great for a brunch.

16	slices cinnamon raisin bread	1	cup heavy cream
1	stick unsalted butter, melted	1	tablespoon vanilla extract
4	whole eggs		Confectioners' sugar
2	egg yolks	1	cup fresh blueberries, sliced
¾	cup sugar	1	cup raspberries, sliced
3	cups milk	1	cup strawberries, sliced

Preheat oven to 350°. Brush both sides of each bread slice with butter and arrange in rows in a buttered 9 x 12-inch baking dish. In a large bowl, beat together the whole eggs and egg yolks. Whisk in the sugar, milk, cream, and vanilla. Strain the custard mixture over the bread slices, making sure that each piece is evenly moistened. This can sit in the refrigerator overnight. Place the baking dish in a roasting pan and pour in enough warm water to reach halfway up the sides of the dish. Bake in upper third of the oven for 25 to 60 minutes or until the top is lightly browned and the custard is set. Transfer to a rack and let rest for about 15 minutes. Cut into squares; sprinkle with powdered sugar and serve with the berries.

Pat Chapman

Crispy French Toast

2 eggs
¼ cup milk
1 cup crunched corn flakes
6 thick slices of day-old French
    bread

¼ teaspoon ground cinnamon
½ teaspoon vanilla extract
   Dash of salt

Combine eggs, milk, cinnamon, and vanilla in blender. Dip bread slices in egg mixture until thoroughly moistened. Drain off excess liquid and place bread in corn flake crumbs. Sprinkle both sides lightly with crumbs. Heat oven to 450°. Place on buttered baking sheet and bake 5 minutes on each side.

French Toast Decadence

16 slices firm bread
3-4 ounces cream cheese
   Cinnamon and granulated sugar
1 cup brown sugar
1 stick butter or margarine

¼ cup maple syrup
6 large eggs
1¾ cups milk
1 teaspoon vanilla
   Berries and sour cream for garnish

Arrange bread in 11 x 17-inch pan. Spread 8 slices with cream cheese and sprinkle with cinnamon and granulated sugar. Top with second slice of bread to make a "sandwich." Cut in half diagonally, or to fit into the pan. Before placing bread in pan, combine brown sugar, butter and maple syrup. Cook until well-blended and dissolved for about 5 minutes. Fit sandwiches into pan on top of mixture. Blend eggs, milk and vanilla in blender. Pour over bread. Cover and let set at least 45 minutes or overnight in the fridge. Bake at 350° for 30 to 40 minutes. Remove pieces from pan and flip to caramel side up. Top with berries and a small dollop of sour cream. Serve immediately.

Serves 8

This is a great decadent breakfast. Recipe changes with types of bread. Cinnamon raisin and sourdough are great.

Pannikin's French Toast

4 eggs	½ cup orange juice
½ cup heavy cream	

Mix ingredients in blender. Soak thick slices of French bread in mixture for 10 minutes. Brown on buttered griddle quickly. Then bake in oven at 350° for 15 minutes.

Carol Sims—from the chef at Pannikin's Restaurant in LaJolla, California.

Popovers

1 tablespoon unsalted butter, melted	½ teaspoon salt
1 cup all-purpose flour	2 large eggs
	1¼ cups milk

Heat oven to 450°. (Lightly grease and flour a popover tin or use the coated popover pans. These popover pans are wonderful. You don't need to use any grease. Popovers cook beautifully. One of my most favorite kitchen investments.)

Mix all ingredients in blender. Fill the popover cups two-thirds to three-quarters full. Bake for 15 minutes. Reduce temperature to 350° and bake 20 minutes more until well browned and crusty. Remove from oven. Puncture the sides with a sharp knife to let steam escape and serve immediately. Great with honey.

Carol Sims

Every good cause and every generous object gains strength,
and purpose, and determination when it is heated over a cup of tea.

~James Hurnard

Gingerbread Pancakes or Muffins

2	eggs	1	teaspoon ground ginger
½	cup butter	1	teaspoon cinnamon
1	cup molasses	½	teaspoon nutmeg
¾	cup buttermilk	½	teaspoon cloves
½	cup coffee	1½	teaspoons baking powder
2	cups flour	1	teaspoon baking soda

Mix with beater until smooth and make as pancakes on griddle or put in muffin cups and bake at 350° for 25 minutes.

Apple Streusel Muffins

Batter:

1½	cups flour	¼	teaspoon salt
½	cup sugar	2	large eggs
2	teaspoons baking powder	1	cup sour cream
1	teaspoon ground cinnamon	¼	cup butter, melted
¼	teaspoon ground allspice	1	cup diced unpeeled tart apple
¼	teaspoon baking soda		

Topping:

½	cup chopped walnuts	2	tablespoons butter
¼	cup flour	¼	teaspoon ground cinnamon
3	tablespoons sugar		

Heat oven to 375°. Grease muffin pan. Put streusel topping ingredients into a medium size bowl. Mix with fork; crumble with fingers until mixture looks like chopped walnuts. Mix flour, sugar, baking powder, cinnamon, allspice baking soda, and salt in a large bowl. Break eggs into another bowl. Add sour cream and melted butter; whisk until blended. Stir in diced apples. Pour egg mixture over flour mixture and fold in just until dry ingredients are moistened. Pour batter into muffin cups. Top each muffin with 2 teaspoons of streusel topping. Bake for 20 to 25 minutes or until browned. Remove from pans and let cool for at least 1 hour before serving (if you can wait that long).

Pat Chapman

Ooey Gooey Coffee Cake

This yummy concoction is one of those delights you eat for breakfast on your birthday or on Christmas morning when you won't feel guilty.

1½ sticks melted butter	1 tablespoon cinnamon
1½ cups brown sugar	2 cans (refrigerated buttermilk
1 cup chopped pecans	canned biscuits, quartered)

Quarter each biscuit and put in a bowl. Mix the other ingredients together and pour over biscuits and toss. Then put the ooey gooey biscuits in a greased Bundt pan. Bake at 350° oven for 30 minutes. Remove from pan after it has cooled for 10 to 15 minutes.

Blueberry Muffins

1 cup buttermilk (I use milk when I don't have buttermilk)	½ teaspoon salt
	1 teaspoon soda
1 cup bran flakes, raisin bran, or frosted mini wheats cereal	1 egg, beaten
	¼ cup melted butter or canola oil
¾ cup sugar	1 cup fresh or frozen blueberries
1¼ cups flour	

Pour buttermilk over cereal in small bowl and let stand while you're mixing the rest of the recipe. Mix by hand eggs, oil and then rest of dry ingredients. Then add buttermilk/cereal mixture. Pour batter into sprayed muffin pans and bake at 400° for 20 minutes.

Carol Sims—very moist and easy to make.

A joy worth repeating, again and again, warm conversation, tea, and a friend.

~Miss Madeline

Broccoli Cornbread

2	packages Jiffy cornbread	2-3	sticks melted butter
1	cup cottage cheese	1	(10-ounce) package chopped
4	eggs, beaten		broccoli, thawed and drained

Mix together; pour into 9 x 13-inch pan and bake 45 minutes to 1 hour at 325°. (Add a little milk if batter is too stiff.)

Clifteen Samuelson and Susan McCormick

Cypress Inn Muffins

3	cups sugar	2	teaspoons salt
1	(15-ounce) box Raisin Bran Cereal	5	teaspoons baking soda
5	cups flour (not self-rising)	1	teaspoon nutmeg
1	cup oil	1	teaspoon cloves
4	eggs	1	teaspoon cinnamon
1	quart buttermilk	2	teaspoons vanilla

Preheat oven to 400°. Mix together all dry ingredients. Then add other ingredients and mix well. Fill muffin pan ½ full and bake for 15 minutes. The batter will keep for 4 weeks in the refrigerator.

Julia Brown

Poppy Seed Muffins

Everyone loves these—you can keep the batter in the fridge for a few days.

3	cups flour	1½	cups milk
2¼	cups sugar	3	eggs
1½	teaspoons baking powder	1	teaspoon almond extract
1½	teaspoons salt	1½	tablespoons poppy seeds
1½	cups vegetable oil		

Mix all ingredients. Fill greased muffin tins ½ to ¾ full. Bake 30 minutes in 350° oven.

Carol Sims

Morning Glory Muffins

1¼ cups sugar
2¼ cups flour
1 tablespoon cinnamon
2 teaspoons baking soda
½ teaspoon salt
½ cup shredded coconut
½ cup raisins

2 apples shredded
8 ounces crushed pineapple, drained
2 cups grated carrots
½ cup chopped pecans
3 eggs
¾ cup canola oil
1 teaspoon vanilla

Sift together flour, sugar, cinnamon, baking soda, and salt in a large bowl. Add coconut, fruits, carrots, and nuts. In a separate bowl, whisk eggs with oil and vanilla. Pour mixture into bowl of dry ingredients and blend well. Fill greased muffin tins ¾ full. Bake 350° for 35 minutes. Cool in pan for 10 minutes.

Barbra's Pumpkin Cranberry Bread

2¼ cups flour
1 tablespoon pumpkin pie spice
2 teaspoons baking powder
½ teaspoon salt
2 eggs
1 cup sugar
1 cup brown sugar

1¾ cups (15 ounce can) pumpkin
½ cup canola oil
1 cup fresh cranberries
Chopped pecans or walnuts
3 bananas mashed
2 cups flour
½ teaspoon baking soda

Combine flour, spices, baking powder and salt in large bowl. Combine eggs, sugar, pumpkin and oil in small bowl. Beat until just blended. Add pumpkin mixture to flour mixture. Fold in cranberries. Bake in greased and floured loaf pan at 350° for 55 to 60 minutes or until wooden pick inserted into center comes out clean. Cool in pans for 10 minutes and remove to wire rack.

Barbra Fletcher

Raspberry Streusel Muffins

Just about the best muffins I've ever had. Even tastes great hours later.

1½ cups all-purpose flour	2 teaspoons cinnamon
¼ cup sugar	1 egg, beaten lightly
¼ cup brown sugar	1 stick butter, melted
2 teaspoons baking powder	½ cup milk
¼ teaspoon salt	1¼ cups fresh raspberries

Streusel Topping:

½ cup chopped pecans	2 teaspoons cinnamon
½ cup brown sugar	2 tablespoons butter, melted

Spray muffin pans well with Pam. Sift flour, sugars, baking powder, salt, and cinnamon together in bowl. Make a well in center. Place egg, butter, and milk in well. Stir until just combined with a wooden spoon. Fold in raspberries. Fill each cup ¾ full with batter.

Combine all streusel ingredients and sprinkle on top of each muffin. Bake at 350° until brown and firm, about 20 to 25 minutes. To make glaze, combine ½ cup powdered sugar and 1 tablespoon milk. Drizzle over warm muffins. Serve warm.

Yields 1 dozen

From my friend Pat Chapman

Mexican Cornbread

1 pound can creamed corn	½ teaspoon baking soda
¾ cup milk	1 teaspoon salt
⅓ cup melted shortening	1 (4-ounce) can chopped green chiles
2 eggs slightly beaten	
1 cup cornmeal	1 cup Monterey Jack cheese

Mix all ingredients except chiles and cheese in order given. Pour half of batter into greased 9-inch pan. Top with ½ of cheese and chopped chiles. Spread remaining batter on top of this. Add remaining cheese. Bake 45 minutes at 400°.

Carol Sims

Cream Cheese Squares

We really enjoyed this dish for breakfast at
Claudette & Forrest Sims' wedding in Enterprise, Alabama.

2	(8-ounce) packages Philadelphia Cream Cheese	1	egg yolk
1	cup sugar	1	teaspoon vanilla flavoring

Mix above ingredients.

Spread 1 package crescent roll mix (8) on bottom of 9 x 13-inch pan, slightly greased with Pam. Spread cream cheese mixture on top of crescent rolls. Place another package crescent roll mix (8) on top of mixture. Glaze with slightly beaten egg white.

Mix ¼ cup sugar and ½ teaspoon cinnamon together and sprinkle on top of egg white. Sprinkle 1 package slivered or sliced almonds on top. Bake 30 minutes at 350°. Great for breakfast.

From Brenda Hogan, Claudette Sims' mother.

Nancy's Biscuits

2	cups self-rising flour	¾	cup buttermilk
3	tablespoons Crisco		

Preheat oven 450°. Mix flour and Crisco together with pastry cutter; add buttermilk and stir. Grease pan with Crisco. Wet countertop and put down wax paper. Put flour on wax paper, rolling pin, and dough. Lightly make dough into a ball and roll with rolling pin, not too thin. Cut out with cookie cutter and put on pan. Bake in oven until lightly brown

Helen Maddox

This recipe comes from my 10-yr.-old granddaughter Nancy Lewallen (from a recipe by Jackie Lewallen).

Angel Biscuits

5-6 cups flour	¾ cup Crisco
1 teaspoon baking soda	1 package yeast
1 teaspoon salt	½ cup warm water
3 tablespoons sugar	2 cups buttermilk
3 teaspoons baking powder	

Sift together all dry ingredients. Mix yeast with warm water. Cut Crisco into flour mixture. Add yeast mixture and buttermilk until all flour is mixed. Roll out and cut into biscuits. Bake 350° until brown 10 to 15 minutes. Mixture will keep up to a week-10 days. Better if covered overnight.

Debbie Cooper

Caramel Apple French Toast

1 cup brown sugar	3-4 apples, peeled and thinly sliced
½ cup butter (1 stick)	1 teaspoon vanilla
2 tablespoons light corn syrup	7 eggs
1 cup chopped pecans	1¾ cups milk
8-12 slices (½-inch thick) sweet bread (such as challah or French)	1 (8-ounce) package cream cheese, softened
	Cinnamon and nutmeg to taste

Generously butter or spray 9 x 13-inch glass baking dish. Cook brown sugar, butter and corn syrup in saucepan over medium heat until thickened, about 4 to 5 minutes. Pour hot caramel sauce into dish and sprinkle on the pecans. Mix eggs, milk, and vanilla in blender. Place half of the bread slices on top of pecans. Spread cream cheese on top of bread. Cover with apples and pour on half the egg mixture. Layer remaining bread and cover with the rest of egg mixture. Sprinkle with spices to taste. Bake at 350° for 50 to 60 minutes. Serve with whipped cream.

Carol Sims

Soups & Salads

Potato Soup

4-6 medium potatoes
3 tablespoons butter
2 teaspoons salt
½ teaspoon pepper

3 cups milk
½ of one small onion, grated or finely chopped
Parsley to garnish

Slice peeled potatoes thinly and cook in water to cover until tender. Drain off the water, and with a potato masher, mash the potatoes until they are smooth. Add all other ingredients except parsley and quickly bring to a boil. Stir constantly to prevent sticking. Immediately reduce heat and simmer for about 15 minutes. Add parsley as a garnish, along with grated Cheddar cheese, bacon bits, and sour cream.

Carol Sims

Cheese Soup

¼ cup butter
½ cup diced onions
½ cup sliced carrots
¼ cup flour
1½ tablespoons cornstarch
½ cup sliced celery
4 cups chicken stock (4 cans Campbell's chicken stock)

4 cups milk (room temperature)
⅛ teaspoon baking soda
1 pound Old English processed cheese, cut up (Kraft)
1 teaspoon salt
1 tablespoon dried parsley
Dash of cayenne pepper, black pepper, and paprika

Melt butter and sauté vegetables. Stir in flour and cornstarch; cook until it bubbles. Add chicken stock and milk. Stir and gradually add cheese until blended. Add seasonings.

Linda Dryden

Creamy Zucchini Soup

1	medium onion, chopped	12	ounces cream cheese, soften and cubed
2	tablespoons butter		
3	pounds zucchini, sliced	½	teaspoon nutmeg
3	carrots, sliced	1	teaspoon basil
6	cups chicken broth		Salt and pepper to taste

In a stockpot, sauté onion in butter. Add zucchini, carrots and chicken broth. Cook for 15 to 20 minutes or until vegetables are just tender. Purée half of the zucchini mixture in a blender or food processor. Repeat with remaining half. Be careful not to burn yourself. Return puréed mixture to sauce pan. Add cream cheese, nutmeg, and salt and pepper to taste. Stir over low heat until cream cheese is melted. Do not overcook. Garnish with additional nutmeg.

Vegetable Beef Soup

2   pounds beef chuck (cut into cubes)

Cook beef covered with water in a big pot on low until meat is tender (about 2 hours).

Add:

2	large cans crushed tomatoes	1	(10-ounce) package frozen cut okra
1	(16-ounce) package frozen mixed soup vegetables	1	(10-ounce) package frozen corn
1	(16-ounce) package gumbo soup vegetables	1	(10-ounce) package frozen lima beans
			Fresh carrots cut-up

Let this simmer 1 hour covered. Add ½ to 1 cup rice (uncooked) or potatoes or noodles. If too thick, add tomato juice or V-8 juice or beef bouillon cubes and water. Add salt, pepper and celery salt. Freezes well.

Helen Maddox

This is better the second day!

French Market Soup

1	large frying chicken	1	quart tomatoes, canned
1	pound smoked sausage sliced	2	onions, chopped
1	tablespoon salt	2	cloves garlic
	Ham hock or bacon strips	6	stalks celery, cut-up
	Bouquet garnish	1	large green pepper sliced
½	teaspoon cayenne pepper	2	cups Nine-Bean soup mix

Wash dry bean mixture, drain, add water to cover with 1 tablespoon of salt and baking soda (secret to preventing unwanted side affects from the beans). Soak overnight. Drain. To the drained bean mixture, add 2 quarts water, ham hock, bouquet garni. Cover and simmer 3 hours. Add all other ingredients except sausage and chicken. Simmer uncovered 1½ hours. Add sausage and chicken and simmer until chicken is done. Remove chicken from pot and debone and cut into small pieces. Return to the pot. Add salt. Ten minutes before serving add 2 tablespoons of parsley.

Carol Sims

We used to include this soup in our Christmas Eve menu with fresh biscuits.

Taco Soup

1	pound lean ground beef	1	can mild Rotel tomatoes
1	pound ground turkey	1	can kidney or pinto beans
1	onion, chopped and drained	1	(20 ounce) can hominy
2	cans diced tomatoes	2	cups water

Brown ground beef and turkey with onion; drain. Cook all ingredients in stockpot 30 to 45 minutes. Serve with cheese and chips.

Clifteen Samuelson

1886 Chicken Soup

⅓ cup butter	1 cup warm cream
¾ cup flour	½ teaspoon salt
6 cups chicken stock	¼ teaspoon pepper
1 cup warm milk	2 cups diced chicken

Melt butter and add flour and cook over heat until well blended but not browned. Gradually add 2 cups hot chicken stock, warm milk, and cream, blending well. Cook slowly stirring frequently until thick. Add remaining 4 cups stock and diced chicken. Heat to boiling. Season with salt and pepper. Serve with toasted almonds.

Corny Ham Chowder

8 slices bacon	1 (16-ounce) can whole kernel corn
2 cups chopped onions	1 (16-ounce) can cream style corn
4 cups chopped potatoes	2 cups half-and-half
½ cup celery, chopped	Black pepper and salt to taste
2 cups chicken broth	Parsley
3 cups cubed ham	

Fry bacon in skillet until crisp. Drain and reserve ¼ cup grease. Sauté onions in bacon grease until tender. Combine potatoes, celery slices, sautéed onions and broth in large saucepan. Bring mixture to boiling, cover and simmer until potatoes are tender. Stir in cubed ham and both cans of corn; add half and half. Heat thoroughly; season to taste. Serve with crumbled bacon and parsley sprinkled on top. 8 servings.

Ginny Sims Craft (my mother-in-law, who spoiled my husband with delicious home-cooking)

Carol's 1999 Green Salad

*This was a hit at Jonathan and Ben's
combined college and high school graduation celebration!*

1	bag prepared cut-up lettuce (Hearts of romaine, bib or baby spinach)	1	cup sliced fresh strawberries or fresh sliced pear or dried cranberries
¾	cup crumbled blue cheese or goat cheese	½	cup sliced green bell pepper
		½	cup sliced red bell pepper
		1	cup sugared or mapled roasted pecans

Combine ingredients and toss right before serving with Celery Seed Dressing on page 60.

Carol Sims

Ann's German Potato Salad

*This is the potato salad I grew up eating. After I was first married,
I tried to make this without knowing the recipe and mistakenly used vinegar
instead of oil and lemon and created quite a disaster.*

6	large potatoes		Juice of 1 large lemon
1	stalk of celery, chopped	½	cup canola oil
1	white onion, chopped		Salt and pepper to taste

Peel and boil the potatoes until tender. Cut up and mash a little bit in a large bowl. Add chopped celery and onions. Sprinkle with juice of one large or two small lemons. Toss with canola oil and salt and pepper. You may also add fresh basil and cilantro. Let sit in the refrigerator before serving. If it seems too dry, add more oil the following day. Nice refreshing potato salad.

Ann Burney Eidschun Shotmeyer—my mother who taught me the love of cooking.

Sugared Pecans

⅓ cup butter	¼ cup sugar
¼ teaspoon nutmeg	¼ cup ground ginger
½ teaspoon cinnamon	1 pound pecan halves

Melt butter on low heat in a saucepan. Stir in the sugar and spices and mix well. Pour heated mixture over nuts in a large pan and mix to coat the nuts well. Bake at 275° for 30 minutes. Store in an airtight tin or freeze.

Carol Maddox Forrester's Pasta Salad

1 pound cooked pasta	McCormick Salad Supreme
Zesty Italian Dressing (Kraft)	Seasoning

Cook pasta. Drain and add any vegetables you desire (broccoli, carrots, cauliflower, onion, green peas, tomatoes) along with chicken or shrimp. Mix with salad dressing and salad supreme and chill.

Carol Maddox Forrester (my cousin Helen Maddox's daughter)

Chicken Salad

4 cups cooked, cubed chicken breasts	½ cup chopped walnuts
8 celery ribs, chopped	½ cup Celery Seed Dressing (see recipe on page 60)
6 green onions, thinly sliced	½ cup Hellmann's mayonnaise
¼ cup capers, undrained	¼ teaspoon curry powder

Toss all ingredients together and refrigerate and allow flavors to blend before using.

Carol Sims

Cranberry Salad

1 (3-ounce) box strawberry jello	1 can jellied cranberry sauce
1 (3-ounce) box black cherry jello	1½ cups boiling water
1 (15-ounce) can crushed pineapple	

Dissolve the jello (2 boxes) using 1½ cups boiling water. Mash cranberry sauce, then add pineapple to jello. Pour in pan and chill.

Holiday Salad

1 package Knox gelatin	1 pound box frozen strawberries mashed
⅓ cup cold water	
2 cups boiling water	1 small can crushed pineapple (juice too)
2 packages cherry jello	
1½ cups cold water	1 (8-ounce) package cream cheese, softened
3 large bananas mashed	
	1 (8-ounce) carton sour cream

Mix Knox gelatin with cold water. Mix boiling water with cherry jello, cold water, bananas, strawberries and pineapple. Pour half mixture into mold. Let congeal. Mix cream cheese with sour cream. Spread with cream cheese and sour cream mixture. Pour remainder of jello mixture on top.

Helen Maddox

I put in freezer for about 15 minutes before pouring cheese mixture. This can also be made in 13 x 9-inch casserole.

*You can't get a cup of tea large enough
or a book long enough to suit me.*

~C.S. Lewis

Killer Salad

4	cooked chicken breasts, cubed	½	head cabbage thinly sliced
¾	cup sliced almonds	½	head shredded lettuce
½	stick butter (¼ cup)	1	bunch green onions sliced
⅓	cup sesame seeds		(tops and bottoms)
1	package Chicken Ramen	½	cup green bell pepper, chopped
	Noodles, shredded and crushed	½	cup red bell pepper, chopped

In a large skillet, melt butter and lightly brown almonds, sesame seeds and Ramen noodles (without flavor pack). Let mixture cool and store in zip lock bag. Toss lettuce, cabbage, green onions, and bell peppers. Right before serving add to this mixture the almond, sesame seed, and crushed noodle mixture. Toss the salad with the following dressing and serve immediately:

Dressing:

½	cup canola oil	3	tablespoons soy sauce
3	tablespoons sugar	1	teaspoon salt
3	tablespoons balsamic vinegar	½	teaspoon pepper

You may choose to add the Ramen noodle seasoning packet in the dressing. This dressing can be stored in the refrigerator for 10 days.

Inspired by Linda Sims, Penny Gressett, and DeeDee Sims

Famous House Salad Dressing

Equal amounts of ketchup, oil, sugar, and vinegar. Blend and add your favorite flavors: onion flakes, celery seeds, and garlic powder.

Linda Sims

Celery Seed Dressing

Our family's favorite. Everyone will go crazy over this!

⅔	cup sugar	⅓	cup honey
1	teaspoon dried mustard	⅓	cup apple cider vinegar
1	teaspoon paprika	1	tablespoon fresh lemon juice
1	teaspoon celery seed	1	teaspoon grated onion (fresh)
¼	teaspoon salt	1	cup canola oil

Mix all ingredients in a blender until well mixed. Store in the refrigerator for 4 weeks.

Judy Hollatz's mother

Mama's Salad Dressing

½	cup Wesson oil (Canola)	6	small green onions (including some of the green tops-do not substitute)
½	fresh lemon juice		Salt and pepper to taste

Squeeze lemons and add oil. Chop onions and part of green tops. Add salt and pepper. Mix well. This is better the next day. Will stay fresh in the refrigerator 3 to 4 weeks. Gets better with age.

Helen Maddox—my mother Helen Burney Grant's recipe (Carol's Aunt)

I imagined one day what I might be a perfect representation of the importance of tea in history or culture. I saw in my mind's eye Queen Victoria time-traveling to a meeting with Ghenghis Khan. They had all the banners and retinue; sitting outdoors in China at a simple table they drank tea. Tea is the drink of choice for Barbarians and sophisticates, West and East, Australian outbackers or city fold. It is a universal in most of the Old World and much of the New.

~Bob Sims

Layered Chicken Salad

1	head lettuce (bite-size dry pieces)	2	cups cooked diced chicken
½	onion, chopped	1	pint mayonnaise
1	cup chopped celery	1	cup mozzarella
1	can water chestnuts, sliced	½	cup Parmesan cheese
1	box frozen peas, not defrosted	6	pieces bacon, cooked and
3	teaspoons sugar		crumbled

Combine lettuce, onion, celery, water chestnuts, and peas; sprinkle with sugar. Layer ingredients in casserole dish. Cover with chicken. Spread mayonnaise on top. Layer mozzarella (shredded) cheese on top of mayonnaise, Parmesan cheese and crispy bacon on top. Cover with Saran wrap and keep in refrigerator overnight.

This is an easy and delicious luncheon menu served with hot rolls.

Macaroni Salad

8	ounces macaroni	½	pound sharp cheese, grated
1	cup mayonnaise	¼	cup chopped onion
1	can mushroom soup	¼	cup chopped bell pepper
1	small jar pimento	1½	stacks saltine crackers, crushed
1	small jar sliced mushrooms	1½	sticks margarine, melted

Cook macaroni and drain. Add remaining ingredients, except crackers and margarine. Pour into casserole dish. Mix crackers and margarine together and pour over other ingredients. Bake 350° degrees until crackers are browned and the casserole is bubbling, about 20 to 30 minutes.

Brenda Hogan, Claudette Hogan's (Forrest Sims' wife) mother

Main Dishes

Jalapeño Chicken

Great for dinner parties!

½   cup chopped onions
2   tablespoons butter
1   (10-ounce) package frozen chopped spinach, cooked and drained
6   jalapeño peppers, chopped
1   pint sour cream

2   cans cream of chicken soup
4   green onions (tops only)
½   teaspoon salt
    Small package Doritos
4-6 cups cooked chicken breasts
2   cups grated Monterey Jack cheese

Sauté onions and jalapeños in butter. In a large bowl, blend in spinach, jalapeños, sour cream, soup, onion tops, and salt with onions and jalapeño mixture. In a large Pyrex dish, alternate layers of Doritos, chicken, spinach mixture and cheese. Layer again, ending with cheese. Sprinkle crushed Doritos on top. Bake at 300° for 1 hour if frozen. If unfrozen, bake at 350° for 30 to 40 minutes.

Carol Sims

Chicken or Turkey Casserole

In greased shallow casserole, arrange in layers: ⅔ cup Pepperidge Farm Cornbread Crumbs, 1 package frozen French-cut string beans (partly cooked), 2 or 3 tablespoons blanched slivered almonds, then sliced or cubed chicken or turkey. Pour over all with 1½ cups canned gravy, (leftover Thanksgiving gravy, or 1 can cream of mushroom soup blended with ½ cup milk). Now moisten 1⅓ cups stuffing crumbs with ¼ cup hot water and 2 tablespoons melted butter. Spread over casserole. Bake in hot oven at 400° for 30 minutes.

Carol Sims

Great for leftover turkey at Thanksgiving.

Chicken and Biscuit Casserole

All my boys love this one! Great to take to friends just home from the hospital.

1	whole chicken or 6 chicken breasts	1	white potato cut up into cubes
	Salt and pepper	1	cup chopped onions
3	cups chicken broth	⅓	cup butter
1½	cups chopped celery	½	cup flour
1	cup sliced carrots	½	teaspoon poultry seasoning
		1½	cups milk

Place chicken, water, celery, onions, and carrots in a 4-quart Dutch oven. (I use a pressure cooker.) I season chicken and vegetables with salt, pepper, and basil. After chicken is tender, debone cutting into bite-size pieces, reserving the broth. Melt ⅓ cup butter in a large saucepan. Stir in flour and seasonings until smooth. Remove from heat and gradually stir in milk and reserved broth. Bring to a boil, stirring constantly. Boil and stir for 1 minute until thick. Stir in reserved veggies and chicken. Pour into casserole dish.

Biscuit Topping:

Combine 1 cup flour, ½ cup shredded Cheddar cheese, 1½ teaspoons baking powder, and ¼ teaspoon salt. Cut in 3 tablespoons butter until mixture resembles coarse crumbs. Stir in ½ cup milk until moist. Drop biscuits by tablespoons onto chicken casserole. Bake for 20 to 25 minutes in 425° preheated oven until biscuits are golden brown.

Carol Sims

Chicken Allouette

4	boneless, skinless chicken breasts	1	container of Herb & Garlic Allouette
1	Pepperidge Farm pastry sheet, thawed		

Roll out pastry sheet and cut into four sheets. Spread ¼ of Allouette into pastry, top with chicken breast. Fold pastry and pinch seam. Place seam down on baking sheet. Bake at 425° for 20 minutes. Serve with wild rice and mixed green salad.

Cathy Present

Main Dishes

Turkey and Wild Rice Casserole

1	(6-ounce) package long-grain and wild rice mix	1	tablespoon cornstarch
½	pound bulk pork sausage	1	cup milk
1	cup sliced fresh mushrooms	1	tablespoon Worcestershire sauce
½	cup sliced celery	3	cups chopped cooked turkey
½	cup chopped green onions	1	cup dried cranberries
		½	cup walnuts

Prepare rice mix according to package directions and set aside. Cook sausage, mushrooms, and celery in a large skillet until sausage is browned, stirring to crumble meat. Drain sausage mixture, reserving 1 tablespoon drippings in skillet. Set sausage mixture aside. Add cornstarch to drippings in skillet, stirring until smooth. Cook 1 minute, stirring constantly. Gradually add milk and Worcestershire sauce; cook over medium heat, stirring constantly until mixture is thickened. Combine rice, sausage mixture, sauces, turkey, and cranberries. Spoon mixture into a lightly greased baking dish. Can store in refrigerator for 2 days or freezer for 2 weeks. Bake thawed uncovered at 350° for 40 to 45 minutes.

Judy Hollatz

Annie Earl's Hawaiian Chicken

1	large can crushed pineapple	1	tablespoon soy sauce
2	tablespoons cornstarch	¼	teaspoon ginger
1	cup sugar	1	chicken bouillon cube
¾	cup vinegar		

Brown chicken and put in pan. To make the sauce: drain pineapple, add water to the juice to make 1¼ cups liquid. Combine sugar, soy sauce, vinegar, cornstarch, ginger, bouillon to mixture. Thicken over heat in a saucepan. Boil for 2 minutes, stirring constantly. Add the pineapple. Pour over chicken and bake at 350° for 1 hour.

Linda Sims

Chicken & Artichoke Casserole
Delightful for luncheons.

1	box chicken Rice-a-Roni	2	jars marinated artichoke hearts (Progresso)
2	bunches green onions, chopped	4	cooked chicken breasts cut up
½	cup chopped green peppers	½	cup mayonnaise
4	ounces sliced black olives		

Cook Rice-a-Roni slightly. Chop up artichoke hearts and save liquid. Combine all ingredients together except mayonnaise and artichoke juice. Put mixture in casserole baking dish. Combine juice with mayonnaise and whisk together. Pour mayonnaise mixture over casserole. Let set overnight. Bake 35 to 40 minutes at 350°.

This is also delicious cold.

Carol Sims

Chicken Divan

4	chicken breasts	2	tablespoons butter
2	cups water	3	tablespoons flour
	Salt and pepper		Milk
1	package frozen broccoli spear or fresh broccoli		Grated Parmesan cheese

Simmer chicken in water covered with 1 teaspoon salt for about 45 minutes or until tender. Save broth. Remove meat from bones in large pieces, cut into long slices. Cook broccoli until just tender, drain and put in shallow casserole. Melt butter in top part of double broiler or saucepan. Stir in flour. Measure chicken broth and add enough milk to make 2 cups. Gradually stir into butter and flour mixture. Cook over boiling water or on low heat in saucepan, stirring constantly until thickened. Add seasoning. Cover broccoli with chicken pieces, then sauce. Sprinkle with cheese. Bake at 400° for about 12 minutes.

Carol Sims

This is a great casserole dish for company, because it can be made ahead of time. Serve with white rice.

Chicken Tetrazzini

4 ounces thin spaghetti
  (break into 2-inch pieces)
2 cups chicken cooked and cut into
  chunks
¼ cup diced pimento
½ small onion diced

1 can cream of mushroom soup
½ cup chicken stock
½ teaspoon salt
½ teaspoon pepper
½ pound grated sharp Cheddar
  cheese

Cook chicken; cook spaghetti and drain. Grate onion. Mix all ingredients together in bowl and put into casserole. Double this recipe and put in 3-quart casserole dish for about 10 servings. Bake 350° for 45 minutes. Freezes well.

Helen Maddox

Linda's Hot Peanutty Chicken Salad

My son Scott's favorite—I serve it to company often.

¾ cup chopped peanuts
¼ cup chopped green pepper
2½ cups cooked, cut-up chicken
¼ chopped green onion
1½ cups cooked rice
¾ cup mayonnaise
  (not salad dressing)

1 can mushrooms
1 can cream of mushroom soup or
  cream of chicken
1 cup shredded cheese
  Salt and pepper to taste

Mix everything together except ¼ cup peanuts and cheese. Put in a 2-quart casserole and sprinkle peanuts and cheese on top. Bake 400° for 30 to 40 minutes.

Yields 6 servings

Linda Sims

Javanese Dinner

Great for serving a crowd. Serve as a buffet in the order given!

On each dinner plate place:

Steamed rice

Stewed chicken pieces in clear gravy (flavored with chicken bouillon and spices or cream of celery, cream of chicken or mushroom soup with curry powder)

Serve the following as a buffet to go on top of chicken mixture:

1	handful chow mein noodles	2	tablespoons shredded coconut
1	tablespoon green onions (finely cup up)	2	tablespoons crushed pineapple (heated)
1	tablespoon celery, cut up	2	tablespoons blanched almonds
2	tablespoons grated Cheddar cheese		

To serve 40 people prepare the following quantities:

5	stewed chickens	5	cups cheese
1¼	gallons rice	5	cups coconut
2	cups onions	5	cups pineapple
3	cups celery	5	cups almonds

Carol Sims

We used to serve this to college students—they loved it.

Ginny's Chicken & Dumplings

3	cups all-purpose flour	1	teaspoon salt
½	cup Crisco		Pinch of baking soda

Add sweet milk to mixture, enough until a soft dough is formed. Chill in refrigerator. Roll on floured surface and cut into thin slices. Drop into boiling chicken broth. Cook for 5 minutes with lid off.

Ginny Sims Craft

Main Dishes

No-Crust Cheese and Chicken Pie

⅓	cup margarine	4	eggs
1	clove garlic, minced	1	cup shredded Monterey Jack cheese
1	cup sliced mushrooms		
1	cup finely chopped onions	1	(10-ounce) package frozen chopped spinach, thawed
1	medium zucchini thinly sliced		
1½	cups diced, cooked chicken	1	(16-ounce) carton cottage cheese

Heat oven to 325°. Melt butter in a large skillet over medium heat. Add garlic, mushrooms, onion, and zucchini; cook for about 2 minutes until just tender. Add chicken and cook for another minute. Set aside. Blend eggs in blender. In a big bowl mix eggs, cheeses, spinach and sautéed vegetables. Pour mixture into a buttered deep 10-inch pie dish. Bake at 325° until set and knife comes out clean, 35 to 40 minutes.

Zippy Honeyed Chicken

⅓	cup butter	4	teaspoons curry powder
½-¾	cup liquid honey	1	chicken (fryer) cut up or 4 chicken breasts
¼	cup mustard		

Melt butter in large shallow pan in oven. Remove from oven and add honey, mustard, and curry; blend well. Roll chicken in mixture and place meaty side down in pan. Bake at 375° for 45 minutes, basting; turn and bake 15 minutes more or until chicken is tender. EASY WAY: Microwave butter and blend with the rest of the ingredients. Place chicken in crock pot and pour over mixture. Cook all day in crock pot. (Cook half the day on high, then on low—depends on how hot your crockpot is—experiment.) Serve with rice.

Carol Sims

The leftover sauce tastes great over rice or served in a pitcher as a gravy for guests.

Main Dishes

Orange-Glazed Chicken Breasts with Sweet Potatoes

Basting Sauce:

¼ cup orange marmalade
2 tablespoons orange juice
1 tablespoon balsamic vinegar

½ teaspoon thyme
¼ teaspoon salt
⅛ teaspoon pepper

Chicken and Vegetables:

4 bone-in skinless chicken breast halves
2 medium dark-orange sweet potatoes, peeled and cubed

1 medium onion, cut into wedges
1 teaspoon olive oil
⅓ cup dried cranberries
¼ cup orange juice

Heat oven to 375°. In a small saucepan, combine all basting sauce ingredients and cook over low heat for 3 to 4 minutes or until marmalade is melted, stirring occasionally. Place chicken breasts in ungreased 15 x 10 x 1-inch baking pan. Brush with half of basting sauce. In medium bowl, toss potatoes and onion with oil; place around chicken. Bake at 375° for 25 minutes. Meanwhile, soak cranberries in ¼ cup orange juice. After 25 minutes, brush chicken with basting sauce and coat vegetables with pan juices. With slotted spoon, sprinkle cranberries over vegetables and drizzle with orange juice. Return to oven and bake an additional 20 minutes or until chicken is fork-tender.

4 servings

When I drink tea, I am conscious of peace, the cool breath of Heaven rises in my sleeves and blows my cares away.

~LuT'ung, Chinese poet

Chicken and Dumplings

*The best southern chicken and dumplings are made from a
whole chicken with skin (it's greasier, but it has that delicious taste).*

1	whole chicken, washed	4	cups Pioneer Biscuit (add to mix ½ teaspoon basil, ½ teaspoon paprika)
1	onion finely chopped		
¾	cup finely chopped celery	1	cup chicken broth
		⅓	cup milk, salt, pepper, and basil

In a large stock pot, sauté onions and celery in 1 tablespoon butter. After
5 minutes, add whole chicken and salt and pepper and cover half way with
water. Cover and cook on stove until tender (30 to 45 minutes). When done,
take out chicken, debone, and cut chicken into 1 to 2-inch pieces. Before
adding chicken pieces back to stockpot, make the dumplings. Cut into 4 cups
Pioneer mix 1 cup chicken broth and ⅓ cup milk. Knead lightly and on
floured board, roll out and cut into 1 x 3-inch pieces that are about ¼-inch
thick. Add water to the stockpot if necessary to make about 4 cups of liquid
(which will have your onions and celery). Bring liquid to a rolling boil and add
dumplings one at a time. After adding them all, lower the heat so it's
simmering for 15 minutes. Near the end of this time, add chicken pieces and
more salt and pepper if necessary.

Carol Sims

Inspired by my friend Mary Durham

Tortilla Chicken & Dumplings

Prepare chicken broth just like recipe above. For dumplings, slice flour tortillas
in strips about 2 inches long and 1-inch wide. When broth is a rolling boil,
drop dumplings into broth and then lower heat and simmer for 20 minutes.

Grilled Vegetable and Polenta Lasagna

¼ cup each: olive oil and balsamic
    vinegar (dark, aged Italian
    vinegar)
3 tablespoons chopped garlic
2 tablespoons each: chopped
    shallots and slivered fresh basil
    Salt and pepper to taste
3 each, sliced lengthwise ¼-inch
    thick: medium-size zucchini
    and yellow squash

1 large eggplant, sliced lengthwise
    ¼-inch thick
1 cup sliced fresh mozzarella cheese
½ cup each, grated: asadero and
    Parmesan cheeses
1 bunch leaf spinach, picked over
    and washed well
3 red bell peppers, roasted and
    peeled
    Polenta (recipe follows)

Marinara Sauce: Freshly grated Parmesan cheese and basil sprigs for garnish. Preheat oven to 350°. Whisk together oil, vinegar, garlic, shallots, basil, salt, and pepper in large mixing bowl. Add zucchini, squash, and eggplant; toss until well coated. Grill vegetables until tender. In a medium size ovenproof baking dish, alternate layers of vegetables with layers of the three cheeses, spinach and bell peppers, seasoning each layer with salt and pepper. Cover pan with aluminum foil and bake about 30 minutes. Spoon about 3 ounces Marinara Sauce over the plate and top with a square of polenta and a square of vegetables. Sprinkle with Parmesan and garnish with a basil sprig.

Makes 6 servings

Polenta

1 quart reduced fat milk
1 tablespoon chopped garlic
2 tablespoons minced shallots

Salt and pepper to taste
2 cups instant polenta

Lightly grease a cookie sheet; set aside. Bring milk, garlic, shallots, salt and pepper to a boil over high heat. Reduce heat to medium-low and whisk in polenta. Stir over low heat about 3 minutes until polenta gets very thick. Pour on to cookie sheet, cover with plastic wrap and press another cookie sheet on top. Let cool, then cut into 3-inch squares. Reheat polenta before serving if made ahead.

From the Inn Above Onion Creek.

Three-Cheese Chicken Enchiladas

2 medium onions (chopped)	4 ounces goat cheese
2 garlic cloves, pressed	24 (6-inch) flour tortillas or 12 (10-inch)
3 tablespoons olive oil	
4 cups chopped cooked chicken	2 cups half-and-half
2 (14½-ounce) cans Mexican-style stewed tomatoes	1 teaspoon chicken bouillon granules
1 (4½-ounce) can chopped green chiles, drained	2 cups grated Monterey Jack cheese
½ teaspoon salt	2 cups shredded Cheddar cheese OR 4 cups Kraft Mexican Four Cheese
2 tablespoons chopped fresh or 2 teaspoons dried cilantro	

Sauté onion and garlic in hot oil in Dutch oven over medium-high heat until tender. Stir in chicken and next 3 ingredients. Bring to a boil: reduce heat and simmer, stirring occasionally for 15 minutes. Stir in cilantro and goat cheese.

Spoon about ¼ cup chicken mixture down center of each tortilla: roll up tortillas and place seam-side down in 2 lightly greased 13 x 9-inch dishes.

Heat half-and-half and bouillon granules in a large saucepan over low heat until granules dissolve. Pour over tortillas.

Bake covered at 350° for 10 minutes; uncover and bake 10 more minutes. Sprinkle with shredded cheese and bake 5 more minutes. Serve with rice.

Pat Chapman

Where there is tea there is hope.

~Sir Athur Pinero (1855-1934),
English playwright

Louis' Chicken Enchiladas with Suizes Sauce

Sauce:

3   pounds fresh tomatillos—wash and husk them—boil until blanched (become pastel green)

Puree tomatillos along with 2 jalapeños and ¼ cup fresh cilantro in food processor or blender. Strain through colander. Cook tomatillos in saucepan with 1 tablespoon cumin and ½ tablespoon oregano, 3 cloves garlic (pressed), and salt to taste. Thicken mixture with a flour paste (flour and water). When thickened, cool in refrigerator. Before using, add 1 part tomatillo sauce to ½ part sour cream until sauce is a light green color.

Filling for enchiladas:

For every pound of chicken breast, add ½ cup Monterey cheese and 1 cup sour cream. Warm tortillas in microwave before filling and rolling. Before laying enchiladas in pan, pour a little bit of sauce in bottom of the pan so the enchiladas don't stick to the pan. Pour sauce over enchiladas and extra cheese. Bake 325° for 1 hour. This can be frozen before adding the sauce.

This wonderful casserole is a specialty of caterer Louis Knox.

Chicken Casserole with Poppy Seeds

4-6 chicken breasts

1   can cream of chicken soup

1   small carton light sour cream

2   tablespoons poppy seeds

Cook chicken until easily removed from bone; cut into bite-size cubes and spread on bottom of casserole. Mix soup and sour cream; pour over chicken. Cover with crushed crackers. Pour melted butter over crackers and sprinkle with poppy seeds. Cook 30 minutes in 350° oven.

Dee Dee Sims

From my mother-in-law Donnie Sims

Cheese Enchiladas

1   pound Red Cascabel Peppers (very hot)

Split these peppers and take out the seeds (wear gloves).

Boil them till they're soft with minimum amount of water. Purée them in blender. (Louis says they are so hot, a hot vapor comes out while pureeing and can cause coughing. After hearing his recipe, I've decided to definitely call him whenever I want theses delicious enchiladas—512-444-0570)

Strain the peppers (red paste) and add 1 tablespoon cumin, ½ tablespoon oregano, 1 tablespoon paprika, and garlic along with salt to taste. Add water and heat with flour paste to thicken. Fill warmed tortillas with white cheese. Pour red sauce over them and more cheese. Bake 325° for 1 hour.

Louis Knox

Carol's Crazy Meatloaf

1	pound ground beef uncooked	1	egg, blended
¼	cup garlic herb bread crumbs	1	teaspoon salt
½	cup chopped bell pepper	½	teaspoon pepper
2	tablespoons dried onion flakes	1	teaspoon basil
¼	cup dried cranberries	¾	cup ketchup
½	cup grated mozzarella cheese	½	cup honey

Mix all the ingredients (except ketchup and honey) together well in a big bowl. I cook this meatloaf in my waterless cookware in a small frying pan on top of the stove covered, leaving a small place for the grease to collect. If you don't have waterless cookware, pat the mixture into a greased loaf pan. Cover the top with the ketchup and then drizzle the honey over the ketchup. Bake at 350° for 30 to 40 minutes until done.

Carol Sims

Mexican Meat Dish

1	cup flour	¼	cup water
½	teaspoon salt	1	can refried beans
1	teaspoon sugar	1	pound ground beef
⅓	cup milk powder	1	small onion
2	teaspoons baking powder	¼	cup diced green pepper
¼	teaspoon cream of tartar	1	package taco seasoning
¼	cup shortening		

Mix flour, salt, sugar, milk powder, baking powder, cream of tartar, and shortening together for a "bisquick" mix. Add the ¼ cup water to the mix: then the can of refried beans. Pat into a 9 x 13-inch pan or on a lipped cookie sheet.

Brown the meat, onion, green pepper, and taco seasoning. Pour this over the crust and bake 350° for 30 minutes. Top with chopped tomatoes and sour cream.

Linda Sims

Good for a crowd!

Mexican Meatloaf

1	pound ground beef	1	package taco seasoning
½	cup chopped onions	1	can chicken and rice soup
¼	cup chopped bell pepper		Shredded cheese for topping
1	can Rotel diced tomatoes		Tortilla chips
1	can cream of mushroom soup		

Brown meat, onions, peppers, and drain. Combine all other ingredients except the cheese and tortilla chips. Spray a pan with Pam. Line the bottom of the pan with a thick layer of tortilla chips. Pour the mixture on top of the chips, then top with cheese. Bake at 350° until hot.

Julia Brown

Down South BBQ

(Crockpot)

4-5 pound pork roast (make sure it fits in crockpot)
3 medium onions
6 cloves garlic
2 cups water
1 bottle BBQ sauce (any kind)

Slice onions. Put one in the bottom of the crockpot with 3 cloves garlic; add roast and other onion and cloves. Add 2 cups water. Cover and cook on low for 8 to 12 hours. I usually cook for 12 hours.

Helen Maddox

Texas Strudel

This can be prepared the day before and baked when ready for your guests.

6 green onions, finely chopped
2 tablespoons butter
  Buttery spray Pam
4 cups chicken breasts, cooked and cubed
½ teaspoon salt
¼ teaspoon pepper
2 tablespoons fresh chopped parsley
1 teaspoon fresh garlic, minced
2 eggs
1½ cups shredded Monterey Jack cheese
2 cups green chilies
½ sliced black olives
½ golden raisins
½ cup slivered almonds
20 sheets phyllo pastry
½ cup butter, melted

Preheat oven to 400°. Sauté onions in butter until tender. In a bowl, combine sautéed onions, chicken, salt, pepper, parley, and garlic. Stir in the eggs, cheese, chilies, olives, raisins, and almonds. In a 9 x 13-inch baking dish, brush butter on the sides and the bottom. Cut phyllo pastry sheets in half width-wise. Begin by laying one piece of phyllo pastry flat in the dish. Spray with buttery Pam and fill with a layer of the mixture. Continue layering with pastry dough sprayed with Pam until 10 layers have been added. Brush the top pastry dough with melted butter instead of Pam. Cut into desired serving sizes before baking. Bake for 35 minutes or until the crust is golden brown. Garnish with a dollop of sour cream and fresh cilantro.

Jo Laughlin

Mock Lasagne

½	pound linguine noodles	1	(8-ounce) package cream cheese
1	tablespoon butter	¼	cup sour cream
1	pound ground beef	½	cup chopped onions
2	(8-ounce) cans tomato sauce	1	tablespoon minced green pepper
1	cup cottage cheese	2	tablespoons melted butter

Cook noodles and drain. Cook beef with butter, then stir in sauce. Combine cottage cheese, cream cheese, sour cream, onions, and green pepper. In 2-quart casserole spread ½ noodles. Then cheese mixture, more noodles. Pour 2 tablespoons melted butter on top. Cover with all meat sauce. Bake 375° for 30 minutes.

Ann Eidschun Shotmeyer

Everyone's Favorite Beef Noodle Casserole
(Helen's Mock Lasagne)

1½	pounds lean ground beef		Dash garlic salt
2	(15-ounce) cans tomato sauce		Salt and pepper to taste
2	cups sour cream	1	cup grated sharp Cheddar cheese
6	small green onions, including green tops	1	(12-ounce) old-fashioned wide noodles
1	tablespoon sugar		

Brown ground meat with dash of garlic salt and 1 tablespoon oil. Drain fat off. Add tomato sauce, salt, pepper and sugar. Cook slowly for 15 to 20 minutes. Mix onions which have been chopped fine with sour cream and set aside. Cook noodles according to package, being careful not to overcook. Layer in 3-quart casserole with noodles, sour cream mixture, beef/tomato sauce. Repeat and sprinkle with cheese. Bake 350° for 35 minutes. Serves 10 or more.

Helen Grant Maddox

Vegetarian Lasagne

Outstanding

10 lasagna noodles	16 ounces Monterey Jack or
1 pound fresh spinach	mozzarella cheese
2 cups sliced fresh mushrooms	Grated Parmesan cheese
1½ teaspoons dried oregano crushed	1 cup grated carrot
2 cups cream-style cottage cheese	1 tablespoon cooking oil
½ cup chopped pitted ripe olives	1 (15-ounce) can tomato sauce
	1 (6-ounce) can tomato paste

Cook lasagna noodles in boiling unsalted water for 8 to 10 minutes or till tender. Drain. Rinse spinach well. In saucepan, cook spinach, without water except the drops that clung to the leaves. Reduce heat when steam forms. Cook 3 to 5 minutes, turning occasionally. In saucepan, cook mushrooms, carrots, and onion in hot oil till tender, but not brown. Stir in tomato sauce, paste, olives and oregano. In greased 13 x 9 x 2-inch pan layer half each of noodles, cottage cheese, spinach, cheese and sauce mixture. Repeat layers reserving some cheese for the top. Bake at 375° for 30 minutes. Sprinkle with Parmesan. Let stand 10 minutes before serving.

Carol Sims

Easy Rump Roast

3-4 pound rump roast	1 can cream of mushroom soup
1 package onion soup mix (Lipton)	1 cup water

Place all in Dutch oven at 300° and cook for about 2 hours or more until tender. Add potatoes, carrots, last 45 minutes. Makes own gravy.

Helen Maddox

Stand-Up Rib Roast

Buy Rib Roast with one rib per person to be served.

Remove from refrigerator at least ½ hour prior to preparing for cooking. Wash it with damp cloth. Trim off excess fat and hard edges. Season roast with salt and pepper and (garlic powder or rub with a cut clove of garlic). Place the roast with fat-side up in roasting pan in oven preheated to 400°. Bake the roast 8 minutes per pound. Turn off oven. DO NOT OPEN OVEN FOR 2 HOURS. Take out of oven and let stand for 30 minutes.

Gravy:
Brown flour in the roasting pan with the roast drippings and add water to thin gravy. Season to taste.

Ginny and Fred Craft

Rémoulade Sauce for Shrimp

1	cup mayonnaise	1	tablespoon horseradish
1	tablespoon chopped onion	½	tablespoon salt
1	tablespoon chopped parsley	½	tablespoon Worcestershire sauce
1	tablespoon chopped celery	1	dash Tabasco sauce
1	tablespoon chopped Dijon mustard	¼	cup Wesson oil
1	teaspoon paprika	1	tablespoon vinegar
			Capers

Mix and refrigerate.

Betty Maddox

Jonathan's Basil Pesto Pasta Sauce

2	ounces fresh basil leaves	½	cup freshly grated Parmesan cheese
½	cup extra-virgin olive oil		
	Salt	2	tablespoons freshly grated Romano cheese
2	tablespoons pine nuts		
2	cloves garlic, peeled		

Preparation:

1. Put the basil leaves, olive oil, pine nuts, garlic, and 1 teaspoon of salt into a food processor or blender and grind until fine and almost creamy.

2. Transfer the mixture to a large bowl and stir in the two grated cheeses.

To serve as a main dish, cut and grill chicken breasts, lightly seasoned to taste. Mix sauce into hot pasta and then add chicken. Must serve immediately for best results.

This sauce goes best with thicker pasta, such as fettuccine, penne, or bow tie, but angel hair also works.

Serves 4 for main dish

Jonathan Sims

You can prepare the sauce ahead of time up to this point and refrigerate or even freeze it. Cover the surface with olive oil to prevent the basil from turning black. I like to make a double batch every time and simply freeze the leftovers for a more informal occasion.

> *I know that nothing is better for them than to rejoice,*
> *and to do good in their lives, and also that every man should eat*
> *and drink and enjoy the good of all his labor—it is the gift of God.*
>
> **~Ecclesiastes 3:12**

Paulette's Long John Silver Fish Batter

½	cup water	1	teaspoon baking powder
½	cup milk		Pinch of salt
1	teaspoon vinegar	1	cup flour

Mix well. Wet fish pieces a little bit so batter will stick. Deep fry until golden brown. Can also be used with de-boned chicken pieces.

Linda Sims

Paul's Grilled Salmon

Dot salmon with butter, brown sugar, and bacon bits. Grill skinside down until just flakey. Don't overcook.

Paul Utnage

Dave's Cedar Planked Salmon

From our Alaskan Cruise

3	tablespoons honey	1¼	teaspoons ground ginger
3	tablespoons olive oil	½	teaspoon ground cloves
3	tablespoons soy sauce	2	cloves garlic
2	tablespoons fresh lime juice		Red pepper flakes
2	tablespoons orange juice		

Mix all ingredients and soak salmon before baking.

Soak plank in marinade for 1 hour before each use. Preheat plank at 400° for 15 minutes. Place salmon on plank and bake at 400° for 10 minutes. Reduce heat to 360° for 20 minutes until flakey.

Ann's Raspberry Veal

Veal prepared for Veal
   Scaloppine (sliced very thin)
3 tablespoons butter
¼ cup Raspberry Wine Vinegar

½ cup heavy cream
1 cup flour (mixed with favorite
   spices)

Bread each piece of veal with flour mixture. Sauté veal in melted butter in a sauce pan on medium high until brown on each side. Add vinegar and after a few seconds, turn the heat down and simmer for 5 minutes. Drizzle cream over simmering veal and cook a few more minutes. This dish cooks very quickly depending on how thick the veal is.

Carol Sims

I watched my mother Ann Eidschun Shotmeyer make this dish. It was never written down until now.

Chicken Fried Venison

Backstrap of venison is the best meat to chicken fry.

The secret is to slice it into fairly thin strips and to double dip.

Mix in a bowl either 1 cup milk, buttermilk, or beer.

In another bowl, mix 1 to 2 cups flour with spices such as paprika, basil, salt, and pepper. Prepare a frying pan with canola oil or butter (if the meat is sliced into very thin pieces like veal scaloppine). Dip the meat in the liquid and then cover with flour mixture. Then dip it again so it's coated completely. Fry the meat quickly in hot oil (medium high) until golden brown. If the meat is backstrap and cut thinly, you don't need to cook it very long.

Thanksgiving Turkey

Guys—remember to read these instructions before Thanksgiving morning, so you have everything you need before the stores close!

Our family loves turkey and wouldn't think of having Thanksgiving or Christmas without it. I'll have to admit, the first time I cooked a turkey for my family, I was very nervous. Since this recipe is for my boys, I'll be very specific. Remember to take the turkey out of the freezer 1½ days before cooking. If your refrigerator has enough room, which mine never does, you can defrost it in there. We usually put the frozen turkey in a cooler out in the garage and let it defrost, checking morning and night to be sure it's not defrosting too quickly or too slowly. It's my husband's job to get up on Thanksgiving morning and prepare the turkey. We usually buy the cheapest and largest turkey we can find. We use the Reynold's cooking bags (turkey size). Wash the turkey and remove the bag of insides. The traditional southern way is to cook these and use them for gravy which I never do. Before placing the turkey (breast-side down) in the bag inside a large roaster or pan, Bob rubs the turkey with the following spices: Malabar pepper, basil, thyme, oregano, dill, cloves, poultry seasoning.

Read the instructions on the cooking bags about how long to bake it. Remember to slit the bag with a few holes before fastening up, so the turkey doesn't blow up on you. We usually cook it slowly at 325° so it's not too dry. When it's done, the little temperature thing will pop up, and the turkey will be golden brown and smell delicious. Drain the juices into a Pyrex container. These can be used to make the gravy.

I make a very simple gravy: In a saucepan mix on medium heat:

2 cups of juices from the turkey (Take as much of the grease off.).

I use Wondra flour (which can be directly put into the hot juices) or I mix 3 tablespoons of all-purpose flour into 2 tablespoons cold water and make a paste. When smooth, I gradually add this to the hot juices and stir until mixed and not lumpy. I add poultry seasoning, basil, pepper, & salt until it tastes just right.

Carol Sims

Tamale Pie

Unsalted butter for baking dish
2 tablespoons extra-virgin olive oil
1 medium yellow onion, coarsely chopped
⅔ medium green bell pepper, coarsely chopped
1 pound ground beef
2 cloves garlic, finely chopped
2 teaspoons hot-chili powder
½ teaspoon dried oregano
1 tablespoon plus ¾ teaspoon coarse salt
Freshly ground black pepper
½ cup (3 ounces) green olives with pimentos, coarsely chopped
½ cup tomato sauce
1½ cups yellow cornmeal
2 bunches scallions, white and light-green parts only chopped, (about 1 cup)
2 tablespoons grated Parmesan cheese

Heat oven to 350°. Butter a 9 x 11-inch baking dish; set aside. In a medium skillet, heat oil over medium-high heat. Add onion and green pepper. Cook, stirring occasionally, until golden brown, 8 to 10 minutes.

Add ground beef, garlic, chili powder, oregano, ¾ teaspoon salt, and black pepper. Cook for 5 minutes, stirring frequently. Stir in olives and tomato sauce. Simmer, uncovered, for 5 minutes.

In a medium saucepan, bring 1½ quarts of water to a boil. Add remaining 1 tablespoon salt. Slowly add cornmeal, whisking constantly, for 5 minutes. Remove from heat and stir in scallions.

Spread half of cornmeal mixture evenly into bottom of prepared pan. Top with meat mixture. Cover with remaining cornmeal mixture; sprinkle with Parmesan. Bake for 30 minutes. Remove from oven and let stand 10 minutes before serving.

Carol Sims

Grilled Meat, Fish, & Vegetables

*We grill a lot of fish and meat at our house. If you have
a Holland grill or one similar, these times may be helpful to you.*

Heat gas grill for 15 minutes and than put the meat on the grill.

Chicken breast—10 minutes on each side

Lamb chops—10 minutes on each side

Tenderloin steaks—10 to 15 minutes on each side for medium rare depending
on how thick they are.

Whole chicken—1 hour without turning breast side down.

Salmon—25 minutes without turning.

Pork tenderloin—25 minutes on each side.

Sliced zucchini and yellow squash—10 to 15 minutes

Inside Outside Ravioli

1	pound ground beef	1	large jar Prego Spaghetti Sauce with mushrooms
1	onion, chopped		
2	tablespoons oil	1	(10-ounce) package frozen chopped spinach
2	well-beaten eggs		
1	cup shredded sharp Cheddar cheese	1	(6-ounce) can tomato paste
		1	(7-ounce) package cooked pasta shells
½	cup bread crumbs		
		¼	cup vegetable oil

Brown beef and onions in oil. Add sauce and paste—simmer. Cook spinach,
saving juice. Mix together (spinach, cheese, eggs, pasta shells, bread crumbs)
and spread on greased casserole. Cover with sauce and bake 350° for 30 minutes.

Carol Sims

Vegetables & Side Dishes

Fresh Green Beans

Snap the green beans (of course the best come from Georgia) by breaking them in half and snapping off the ends and pulling off the strings. I cook my southern style green beans in a pressure cooker. They taste like good ole southern beans that have been cooking all day long. Thanks to Frances Bradley for showing me this trick.

I snap my beans and wash them and place them in the pressure cooker and add about ¼ cup water (depends on how many beans). Don't add too much water. Add salt and pepper to the beans; sometimes I add a tablespoon of sugar and 1 to 2 slices of raw bacon for a real southern flavor. Ten minutes before you want to eat, turn the pressure cooker on high. After it steams, add the pressure top and turn down to low. Cook for about 5 minutes (little longer if the pot is full). Take off the heat and give the pot a minute to cool. When you open, the hot green beans will be ready to eat.

Carol Sims

Black-Eyed Peas

4	cans Trapeys Black-Eyed peas	4	stalks celery, chopped
1	can mild Rotel tomatoes diced	1	pound favorite smoked sausage
1	onion diced fine		(linked) sliced
1	bell pepper cut-up		

Combine all ingredients in big pot and simmer for 3 hours.

Margaret Collis

Green Bean and Corn Casserole

First Layer:

2 (17-ounce) French green beans drained (or frozen beans)	½ cup chopped onion
2 (12-ounce) cans corn	Salt and pepper to taste

Second Layer:

1 can cream of celery soup	1½ cups grated Cheddar cheese
8 ounces sour cream	

Third Layer:

1 roll of Ritz Crackers (crushed)	⅓ cup slivered almonds
½ cup butter (melted)	

Mix first layer and spread into a 9 x 13-inch pan (sprayed with Pam). Mix second layer in a separate bowl, then spread on top of first layer. Mix third layer in separate bowl, then spread on top of second layer. Bake at 350° for 35 minutes or until bubbly, and the center tests to be done.

Helen's Cornbread Dressing

1 medium pan of cornbread	1 teaspoon poultry seasoning
8 slices toasted white bread (hard)	1 teaspoon salt
½ bag dressing mix	1 teaspoon pepper
3 eggs	2 cans chicken broth and pan drippings
2 bunches spring onion and tops chopped	½ cup melted butter
6 stalks celery chopped	1 small can evaporated milk (if needed)
1 teaspoon sage	

Mix all ingredients well and put in 9 x 13-inch greased pan. Cook 350° for about 40 minutes.

Helen Grant Maddox

Carol's Cornbread Dressing

6 cups Pepperidge Farm Cornbread Dressing Crumbs	2 eggs, mixed
1 cup celery chopped	6 tablespoons melted butter
1 cup white onions chopped	1 teaspoon pepper
1 cup fresh chopped mushrooms	½ teaspoon sage
3 cups chicken broth	1 cup pecans (optional)
	1 cup dried cranberries (optional)

Sauté celery, onions and mushrooms in 3 tablespoons butter until tender. Combine all ingredients. To make the dressing more interesting, add 1 cup pecans and ½ cup dried cranberries. Bake at 350° for 30 to 45 minutes.

Carol Sims

Aunt Julia's Sweet Potato Casserole

4 sweet potatoes	2 eggs
1 cup sugar	1 teaspoon vanilla extract
½ cup butter	

Topping:

½ cup butter	½ cup flour
1 cup sugar	1 cup chopped pecans

Boil potatoes until soft. Add sugar, butter, eggs, and vanilla and beat or blend well. Put in greased casserole dish. Cut butter into flour and sugar to make topping. Add pecans and place on top of casserole before baking at 350° uncovered for 30 minutes.

You can put raisins in casserole and marshmallows on top.

Julia Brown

Sweet Potato Casserole

6	sweet potatoes	1	teaspoon vanilla
1	egg	½	teaspoon nutmeg
1	cup brown sugar	½	cup butter
½	teaspoon cinnamon	½	cup heavy cream

Boil sweet potatoes or cook in microwave until tender. Skin potatoes and beat in the rest of the ingredients. (You can use blender.)

Top with marshmallows if you wish and bake at 325° for 30 minutes.

Carol Sims

Company Potatoes

6-9 medium potatoes with jackets		1	cup sour cream
½	cup margarine	1	can cream of mushroom soup or cream of chicken
⅓	chopped green onion		

Topping:

1	cup crushed cornflakes	2	tablespoons melted butter

Boil potatoes with jackets until soft. Cool. Remove jackets and grate potatoes. Heat butter & soup. Add sour cream, cheese, green onion. Mix altogether and place in 9 x 13-inch pan. Sprinkle cornflakes and butter mixture on top of the potatoes. Cover and refrigerate overnight. Bake 350° for 45 minutes.

Linda Sims—from my friend Lynn Sears.

Aunt Julia's Potato Casserole

2	pounds hash brown potatoes thawed
2	cups grated Cheddar cheese
8	ounce sour cream
½	cup chopped onion
¾	cup butter
1	can cream of chicken soup
2	cups cornflakes, crushed

Mix hash browns, cheese, ½ cup butter, onions, sour cream, and soup. Placed in a greased casserole dish. Top with cornflakes and ¼ cup melted butter. Bake at 350° for 45 to 50 minutes.

Julia Brown

Twiced Baked Potatoes

Bake potatoes in oven at 400° for about an hour. I usually bake the number of potatoes that I have people, which will guarantee extras, but my boys always want extra anyway (me too). Be sure to use nicely shaped large potatoes. When the potatoes are right out of the oven, carefully slice them with a sharp knife lengthwise in half. Scoop with a spoon the potato out of the skin, leaving neat potato skins to refill. You'll usually have some bad shells, just toss those. With an electric mixer, beat potatoes until smooth, adding butter and salt & pepper, grated onion flakes, (fresh garlic if desired). After the potatoes are mixed well, you can do several things—add 8 oz. of cream cheese along with ½ to 1 cup sour cream (depends on how many potatoes you have). Beat this up well, then add milk or cream to desired consistency. (One secret is don't add the milk until you get all the lumps out.) I line a cookie sheet with foil and lay my shells all ready to be filled. Carefully scoop potatoes into shells, or you can fill them with a pastry bag. At this point, you can freeze them, but remember to cover well, or you can put them in the refrigerator for later in the day or the next day. Before cooking, spread with grated Cheddar cheese and cook for 30 to 45 minutes at 350°.

Carol Sims

My father-in-law Fred Craft makes the best ones with a similar recipe.

Quick "Real" Mashed Potatoes

*My family has kidded me often because mashed potatoes
are one of my favorite foods, especially real ones. Whenever we dined
out, I asked the waitperson if their mashed potatoes were real. This
recipe is for my boys. It's easy and quick.*

Cook 3 large potatoes in the microwave 4 to 8 minutes on high. (Remember to stick them with knife.) (Red potatoes are really good mashed). It's important to be sure they are tender. Stick a knife in it to test. When the potatoes are done, you can peel the skin off easily while they're hot or include the skin in the recipe. It seems that my mashed potatoes work the best when I use my portable hand mixer instead of my KitchenAid. Mash the potatoes in a large mixing bowl. (Many times I put the bowl in the sink before I turn on the electric mixer, since potatoes start to fly around the room.) You can go the low calorie way by using Mollie McButter or regular butter. Mix in about a ¼ cup or ½ stick of butter and beat adding salt and pepper to taste (onion flakes are good and Malabar pepper). It's important to beat all the lumps out of the potatoes before you add the milk. After you add the milk, it will be too late. Slowly pour in milk while you're beating until it gets to the consistency you desire. If you're not quite ready to eat when you're finished, you can reheat them in the microwave; add a few butter pats.

Carol Sims

Mixed Vegetable Casserole

1 (18-ounce) package frozen mixed vegetables	1 stick butter
	1 medium onion, chopped
1 cup grated Cheddar cheese	1 cup chopped celery
1 cup mayonnaise	1 package saltine crackers, crumbled

Cook vegetables according to the directions on package until they're almost done. Spoon into the bottom of a greased casserole dish. Mix onion, cheese, celery, and mayonnaise together. Place on top of vegetables. Melt butter and mix with crackers. Spread on top of casserole and bake at 350° for 30 minutes.

Claudette Sims

Night Before Mashed Potatoes

8-10 potatoes, peeled	Salt and pepper to taste
8 ounces cream cheese, softened	¼ cup butter
1 cup sour cream	

Boil and drain potatoes. Whip hot potatoes adding cream cheese and sour cream. Continue beating until fluffy and smooth. Add salt and pepper. Place in a buttered 9 x 13-inch baking dish. Dot generously with butter and sprinkle with seasoned salt. Cover with foil and refrigerate. Potatoes can be frozen at this stage and thawed before baking. Bake covered with foil, 15 minutes at 325°. Continue baking uncovered for 20 minutes.

Serves 10 to 12

Poppy's Potatoes

This delicious recipe is from my stepfather Bert Shotmeyer.

4 potatoes (you can use any kind of potatoes)	¼ cup Parmesan cheese
¼ cup butter	Salt and pepper
	1 tablespoon basil

Boil potatoes until done and take the skin off; or bake potatoes until done and scoop potatoes out of skin. Prepare a cookie sheet with foil. Spread small pieces of cooked potatoes evenly over the cookie sheet. Drizzle melted butter over the potatoes. Salt and pepper to taste (also add basil). Sprinkle cheese over butter. Bake in oven at 425° for 15 to 30 minutes until potatoes are golden brown and a little crunchy.

Carol Sims

Wisdom—If you seek her as silver,
And search for her as for hidden treasures;
Then you will understand the fear of the Lord,
And find the knowledge of God.

~Proverbs 2:4-5

Scalloped Potatoes

I serve this on Christmas Eve with honey-baked ham and biscuits.

6-8 raw potatoes peeled and sliced very thinly (Keep sliced raw potatoes in cool water while you're preparing them until you assemble the casserole to keep them from turning brown.)

1 stick of butter
Salt and pepper
¼ cup dried flaked onions
1 cup grated Cheddar cheese
1 cup sour cream
Milk

This recipe can be made for 4 people or many more. The amount of potatoes you prepare determines how big a casserole you'll need. Prepare the greased casserole by layering the following in order:

Layer raw potatoes—sprinkle with flour, salt and pepper, onion flakes and dabs of butter, dollops of sour cream.

Layer Cheddar cheese.

Repeat layers until casserole is filled to the top. Then fill the casserole with milk to the top. Bake at 350° for 1½ hours or until potatoes are tender.

Carol Sims

Carol's Squash Casserole

A Thanksgiving Must!

2 cups cooked squash mashed (yellow)
1 cup sour cream
1 can cream of chicken soup
1 onion chopped

1 small jar sliced pimentos
1 (8-ounce) package Pepperidge Farm herb seasoned stuffing
½ cup butter

Melt butter and sauté onions. Add all ingredients (½ of stuffing) to this mixture. Put in greased casserole. Spread rest of stuffing on top. Bake 350° for 30 minutes.

Carol Sims

Mary's Spinach Delight

2	packages frozen chopped spinach	½	cup sour cream
1	can cream of mushroom soup	2	tablespoons butter
⅓	cup milk	1	teaspoon salt
¾	cup grated Swiss or Cheddar cheese	¼	teaspoon pepper

Cook spinach and drain (steam or microwave). While spinach drains, combine soup with sour cream, butter, and seasonings. Add spinach to sauce in casserole. Top with buttered bread crumbs and bake 350° for 30 minutes.

Linda Sims

Helen's Yellow Squash

2-3	pounds yellow squash	10-12	saltine crackers
2	onions, sliced		Salt and pepper to taste
1	cup sharp cheese grated		

Cook squash and onion until tender. Drain. Mix grated cheese and crushed saltines together. Pour into greased baking dish. Bake 350° 25 to 30 minutes. Freezes well. Serves 6 to 8.

Helen Grant Maddox

Aunt Julia's Creamed Corn

I finally discovered Aunt Julia's famous delicious creamed corn recipe while standing in the reception line at Forrest and Claudette Sims' wedding. One of my favorite southern dishes.

Scrape and milk the corn off 12 ears of fresh uncooked corn. (This involves holding the ear vertical on the cutting board and carefully scraping the corn off the ear with a sharp knife. As you get closer to the cob after cutting most of the corn off, you press with the flat edge of the knife squeezing the juice or milk from the cob.) Put corn, juices, and 1 stick of butter into microwave proof bowl. Cook in microwave on medium high for 20 minutes, stirring half way through the cooking time. Add water if there are not enough natural juices.

Julia Brown

Mary Constable's Corn Pudding

2	cups niblets canned or frozen corn
½	cup chopped green pepper
½	cup chopped onion

Brown the above in 1 tablespoon butter. Make a cream sauce as follows:

1	tablespoon flour
1	teaspoon salt
¼	teaspoon paprika
½	teaspoon dry mustard

Mix well. Take off heat and stir in gradually 1 cup milk. Add 1 beaten egg. Combine corn with sauce in a casserole dish and top with buttered bread crumbs. Bake 375° for 45 minutes.

Linda Sims

Carol's Creamed Corn Pudding Casserole

A must on Christmas Eve with honey baked ham!

1	(12-ounce) can corn niblets	1½	teaspoons seasoned salt
2	(#303) cans creamed style corn	½	teaspoon dried mustard
1	(#303) can whole kernel corn drained	1	teaspoon instant onions
			Dash red pepper
5	eggs slightly beaten	½	cup milk
½	cup sugar	½	cup melted butter
3	tablespoons cornstarch		

Mix together corn and eggs. Combine sugar, cornstarch, seasoned salt, mustard, onion, and pepper. Stir into corn mixture. Add milk and butter. Pour into buttered 3-quart casserole. Bake uncovered 400° oven for 1 hour or until knife comes out clean.

Carol Sims

Vegetables & Side Dishes

Cheese Grits

*We enjoy Callaway Gardens Speckled Heart Grits
or Hoppin John's Grits from Charleston, SC.*

1	cup stone-ground grits	2	cups sharp grated cheese
4	cups water	1	stick butter
1	teaspoon salt	½	milk or cream
2	eggs, blended		Dash Tabasco sauce

To 4 cups of boiling water, add 1 cup of grits and 1 teaspoon salt. Bring to a boil, reduce heat to low, cover and cook for about 20 to 30 minutes, stirring often to prevent sticking. As the grits get thick, add milk or cream for a creamier consistency as they cook. Add cheese, eggs, and seasonings along with butter and put into casserole dish. Bake 1 hour at 325°.

To make fried grits, refrigerate leftover grits. The next morning they will be stiff, so you can slice them into thin pieces. Bread them with flour, salt, paprika, and corn meal and fry in small amount of grease until crispy on the outside.

Carol Sims

Leola's Macaroni and Cheese

*Leola was Helen & Connie Grant's cook when they were growing up.
Whenever I would visit their home, we would always eat in the dining room
with the good china and be served her delicious food. Thank you
Leola for the wonderful meals we all enjoyed.*

1	(8-ounce) package elbow noodles	½	stick butter
2	eggs	2	cups sharp cheese grated
½-¾	cup milk		Salt and pepper

Cook noodles (do not overcook) and drain. Layer in 1½-quart casserole dish—noodles, cheese, noodles, cheese. Mix milk and eggs together and pour over layered mixture. Slice butter and put on top. Bake 350° until firm for about 30 minutes.

Helen Grant Maddox

Cookies & Bars

Ultimate Chocolate Chip Cookies

¾ cup Crisco shortening
1¼ cups light brown sugar
1 teaspoon salt
¾ teaspoon baking soda
1 cup semi-sweet chocolate chips

1 cup coarsely chopped pecans
2 tablespoons milk
1 tablespoon vanilla
1 egg
1¾ cups all-purpose flour

Heat oven to 375°. Combine Crisco, brown sugar, milk, and vanilla in large bowl. Beat at medium speed with electric mixer until well blended. Beat egg into creamed mixture. Combine flour, salt, and baking soda. Mix into creamed mixture just until blended. Stir in chocolate chips and pecan pieces. Drop rounded tablespoonfuls of dough 3 inches apart onto ungreased baking sheet. Bake for 8 to 10 minutes for chewy cookies, or 11 to 13 minutes for crisp cookies.

Makes about 3 dozen cookies

Carol Sims

My favorite chocolate chip cookies.

Jonathan Chocolate Cookies

2 cups all-purpose flour
¾ cup Dutch-process cocoa powder
1 teaspoon baking soda
½ teaspoon salt

1¼ cups unsalted butter
   (2 sticks + 4 tablespoons)
2 cups sugar
2 large eggs
2 teaspoons vanilla extract

Sift together flour, cocoa, baking soda and salt. Cream butter, sugar, and eggs until fluffy, about 2 minutes. Add vanilla and dry mixture. Chill dough for 1 hour. Roll dough into 1-inch balls. Dip in sugar and place on greased baking sheet. Bake at 350° until set for about 8 minutes.

Jonathan Sims' favorite.

Billy's Chocolate Chip Cookies

1 cup butter
1 cup sugar
1 cup brown sugar
2 eggs
1 teaspoon vanilla
2 cups flour
2½ cups oatmeal (old-fashioned)
½ teaspoon salt
3½ teaspoons baking powder
1 teaspoon baking soda
1 (12-ounce) package chocolate chips
1 (4-ounce) bar milk chocolate coarsely chopped
1½ cups pecans

Heat oven to 375°. Cream butter with sugars. Add eggs and vanilla. Combine flour with salt, baking soda, and baking powder. Mix into creamed mixture until blended. Stir in oatmeal, chocolate chips, milk chocolate, and pecan pieces. Drop large Texas size tablespoonfuls of dough 3 inches apart onto ungreased baking sheet. Bake for 19 minutes for large cookies until done.

Bill Smalling

Crunchy Oatmeal Cookies

1 cup shortening
1 cup brown sugar
1 cup white sugar
2 eggs, eaten
1 teaspoon vanilla extract
1½ cups flour
1 teaspoon soda
1 teaspoon soda
1 teaspoon ground nutmeg
1 teaspoon ground cinnamon
1 teaspoon salt
1 cup chopped pecans
3 cups uncooked oatmeal

Cream shortening and sugar. Add eggs and vanilla and beat well. Combine flour, soda, nutmeg, cinnamon, and salt and add to creamed mixture a small amount at a time. Add nuts and oatmeal and mix well. Divide mixture into three parts and shape into rolls. Wrap in waxed paper and freeze until needed. Slice thin and place on greased cookie sheet. Bake at 350° for 8 to 10 minutes.

Yield 4 dozen

Inn Above Onion Creek

Death by Chocolate Cookies

The best chocolate cookie on earth—addictive!

2 packages (12 squares) Baker's Semi-Sweet Baking Chocolate, divided
¾ cup firmly packed brown sugar
¼ cup butter or margarine
2 eggs

1 teaspoon vanilla
½ cup flour
¼ teaspoon baking powder
2 cups chopped nuts (walnuts or pecans)

Heat oven to 350°. Coarsely chop 8 squares (1 package) of the chocolate; set aside. Microwave remaining 8 chocolate squares in large microwavable bowl on HIGH 1 to 2 minutes. Stir until chocolate is melted and smooth. Stir in sugar, butter, eggs, and vanilla. Stir in flour and baking powder. Stir in reserved chopped chocolate and nuts. Drop by ¼ cupfuls onto ungreased cookie sheet. (I don't make them quite that big.) Bake 12 to 13 minutes or until cookies are puffed and feel set to the touch. Cool on cookie sheet 1 minute. Transfer to wire rack to cool completely.

Makes about 1½ dozen or more if you make them smaller

Carol Sims

Black & White Chocolate Chip Cookies

2¼ cups flour
1 teaspoon baking soda
½ teaspoon salt
1 cup unsalted butter
¾ cup sugar
¾ cup brown sugar

2 eggs
2 teaspoons vanilla
1 bag (11½-ounce) mega-size semisweet chocolate morsels
1½ cups chopped walnuts
1 cup white chocolate chips

Heat oven to 375°. Sift flour, baking soda, and salt into bowl. Beat butter; add sugar and beat until fluffy. Beat in eggs one at a time. Add vanilla. On low speed, beat in flour mixture, chocolate morsels and nuts. Drop by heaping tablespoonfuls into ungreased baking sheets. Bake 375° oven for 9 to 11 minutes.

Carol Sims

Cream Cheese Sugar Cookies

1 cup sugar	½ teaspoon almond extract
1 cup softened butter	½ teaspoon vanilla
1 (3-ounce) package cream cheese, softened	1 egg yolk
	2 cups flour
½ teaspoon salt	Colored sugar for decorating

In large bowl, combine all ingredients except flour and colored sugar; beat until light and fluffy. Lightly spoon flour into mixture and mix well. Shape dough into 3 disks. Wrap dough in plastic wrap and refrigerate 1 hour for easier handling. Heat oven to 375°. On floured surface, roll out 1 disk at a time to ⅛-inch thickness. Cut with lightly floured 2½-inch round or desired shape cookie cutters. Place 1 inch apart on ungreased cookie sheets. Decorate if desired before baking. Bake for 6 to 10 minutes or until light golden brown. Frost if desired.

Clifteen Samuelson

These cookies taste great plain!

Forrest's Favorite Lunch Box Cookies

Mix together:

3 cups flour	4½ cups 1-minute oatmeal
1½ cups white sugar	1 teaspoon cinnamon
1½ teaspoons salt	½ teaspoon nutmeg
1½ teaspoons baking soda	

Cream:

1½ cups brown sugar	4 eggs
1½ cups margarine	2 teaspoons vanilla

Add dry mix to creamed mixture. Bake cookies at 325° for 10 to 15 minutes.

Linda Sims

Connie Davis shared this recipe with me. My son Forrest loves them!

Chewy Oatmeal Cranberry Walnut Cookies

1 cup butter softened (2 sticks)	½ teaspoon cinnamon
1 cup brown sugar	½ teaspoon salt
½ cup sugar	3 cups old-fashioned oatmeal uncooked
2 eggs	
1 teaspoon vanilla	1 cup dried cranberries
1½ cups flour	1 cup walnuts coarsely chopped
1 teaspoon baking soda	

Heat oven to 350°. Beat together butter and sugars until creamy. Add eggs and vanilla and beat well. Combine flour, baking soda, and spices; mix well. Mix into creamed mixture. Stir in oatmeal, cranberries, and nuts. Drop by rounded tablespoonfuls onto ungreased cookie sheet. Bake at 350° 10 to 12 minutes or until golden brown.

4 dozen

These cookies remain chewy if kept in the refrigerator.

Carol Sims

Brown Sugar Chews

1 egg white	Pinch salt
1 cup brown sugar	¾ cup pecans
1 tablespoon flour	

Beat egg white until stiff; add brown sugar and continue beating till thoroughly mixed. Stir in flour and salt and fold in pecans. Drop by small teaspoons on buttered cookie sheet. Bake at 325° for 10 minutes. Allow to cool a few minutes before removing from cookie sheet.

Yield 25 cookies

World's Best Cookies

1	cup butter, softened	1	cup vegetable oil
1	cup sugar	1	cup quick-cooking oats
1	cup packed brown sugar	1	cup crushed cornflakes
1	egg	½	cup coconut
½	cup chopped pecans	3½	cups flour
1	teaspoon vanilla extract	1	teaspoon baking soda
1	cup (or more) sifted powdered sugar	1	teaspoon salt

Cream the butter, sugar, and brown sugar in a mixer bowl until light and fluffy. Add the egg and oil; beat well. Stir in the oats, cornflake crumbs, coconut, nuts, vanilla, and a mixture of the flour, baking soda, and salt. Shape into balls; dust with the confectioners' sugar and place on a cookie sheet. Bake at 325° for 12 minutes or until the edges of the cookies are light brown. Cool on the cookie sheet for several minutes. Remove to a wire rack to cool completely. Freezes well.

Carol Sims

A favorite at the Inn Above Onion Creek.

Spritz Cookies

1	cup butter (2 sticks)	½	teaspoon baking powder
¾	cup sugar	1	teaspoon almond extract
1	egg	⅓	teaspoon salt
2½	cups sifted flour		

Cream butter, add sugar, egg, flour and extract. Force through a cookie press (electric is the quickest). Sprinkle with Christmas sprinkles before baking. Bake 400° to 425° 10 to 12 minutes.

Carol Sims

My mother always made these at Christmas—I've continued her tradition. A delightful Christmas tea treat.

Ginger Cookies

1½	cups shortening (Crisco)	2	teaspoons baking soda
2	cups sugar	1	teaspoon ground cinnamon
2	large eggs	1	teaspoon ground cloves
½	cup molasses	1	teaspoon ground ginger
4	cups all-purpose flour		Sugar

Beat all the ingredients at medium speed with an electric mixer until blended. Shape into 1-inch balls and roll in sugar. Place on greased baking sheets and flatten slightly. Bake at 375° for 8 to 10 minutes. Transfer cookies to cool on wire rack.

Yields 7 dozen

Great! Helen Grant Maddox

Cranberry Caramel Bars

Wonderful Thanksgiving or Christmas treat!

2	cups fresh cranberries	½	cup sugar
2	tablespoons sugar (Stir into cranberries and set aside.)	½	cup brown sugar
		1	cup butter, melted
2⅓	cups flour	¾	cup chopped pecans
½	teaspoon baking soda	1	(12-ounce) jar caramel sauce
2	cups oatmeal (old-fashioned)		

Combine 2 cups flour (save the ⅓ cup for the caramel) and the next 4 ingredients. Stir in butter until crumbly. Reserve a cup of this mixture. Press remaining mixture into lightly greased 12 x 9-inch pan. Bake at 350° for 15 minutes. Sprinkle with cranberries and pecans. Stir together caramel and ⅓ cup flour. Spoon sauce over the cranberries. Sprinkle with reserve 1 cup mixture. Bake 25 more minutes.

Almond Macaroons

1 package (7 or 8 ounces) almond paste	¼ teaspoon almond extract
¼ cup flour	2 egg whites
1¼ cups powdered sugar	3 dozen blanched whole almonds

Grease cookie sheet. Break almond paste into small pieces in large bowl. Stir in flour, powdered sugar and almond extract. Add egg whites and beat with electric mixer for about 2 minutes, until smooth.

Place dough in decorating bag fitted with #9 rosette tip. Pipe 1½-inch cookies about 2 inches apart into cookie sheet. Top each with almond. Refrigerate 30 minutes. Heat 325°. Bake about 12 minutes or until edges are light brown. Immediately remove from cookie sheet to wire rack. Cool completely. Store in airtight container.

Christmas Meringue Kisses

(Choose a dry day to make these!)

3 egg whites	Dash salt
⅔ cup sugar	1 teaspoon vanilla extract
1 (6-ounce) package chocolate chips	¼ teaspoon cream of tartar

Preheat oven 350°. Turn off the oven when you put the cookies in. Beat egg whites in bowl with electric mixer. Beat 1 minute; add cream of tartar; beat 1 more minute until mixture becomes foamy white. Increase speed and start adding sugar gradually. Beat until sugar is dissolved and whites are very stiff. Add vanilla extract. Fold in chocolate chips. Put foil paper on cookie sheet and drop by teaspoon onto foil. This recipe should fill two cookie sheets, about 65 drops. Turn oven off and put cookies in oven all night.

Helen Grant Maddox

Our family loves these!

Praline Strips

22-24	graham cracker squares	1	cup butter
½	cup honey	1	cup chopped nuts

Combine honey and butter over medium heat. Let mixture come to a bubbly stage and then cook for 4 to 5 minutes. Remove from heat and stir in nuts. Place crackers in pan and pour mixture over all of them. Bake at 300° oven for 15 minutes. Cut to form strips.

Carol Sims

Hanau Chocolate Mint Squares

*From my friend Nanne Alvarez, who used to
share these with everyone in our office at Christmas time.*

1	cup sugar	½	teaspoon salt
½	cup butter	1	teaspoon vanilla
4	eggs	1	(16-ounce) can Hershey syrup
1	cup flour		

Mix and pour into greased 9 x 13-inch pan. Bake at 350° for 30 minutes.

Mix and spread over cooled cake:

2	cups powdered sugar	2	tablespoons mint extract
½	cup butter		Few drops of green food coloring

Melt and mix 6 ounce chocolate chips and 6 tablespoons butter. Spread over green layer. Chill before cutting into 1-inch squares.

Carol Sims

Forgotten Cookies

3 egg whites
1 cup sugar
¼ teaspoon mint extract

Green food coloring
6 ounces mini chocolate chips

Beat egg whites until soft peaks. Beat in sugar gradually until stiff. Fold in extract, coloring and chips. Drop by teaspoons on cookie sheet covered with paper. Put into oven which has been preheated to 400°. Turn off the heat and leave cookies in oven 4 to 6 hours or overnight.

ITF Brownies

2¼ cups flour
¾ teaspoon salt
¾ cup softened butter
6 eggs
3¾ cups sugar

½ cup + 2 tablespoons cocoa powder
½ cup +1 tablespoon shortening
2¼ teaspoons vanilla

Combine butter, shortening, eggs, vanilla. Mix well. Sift flour, sugar, salt, cocoa powder, and add to mixture. Bake 350° for 25 minutes in 9 x 13-inch pan.

Linda Sims

Chocolate Caramel Brownies

1 box German Chocolate Cake mix
¾ cup melted butter
¼ cup evaporated milk

1 (14-ounce) bag caramels
1 cup nuts
1 cup chocolate chips

Mix cake according to directions. Bake ½ batter at 350° for 15 minutes. Melt caramels with milk and butter. Blend well. Pour over cake while hot. Sprinkle ¾ nuts and all the chocolate chips over caramel. Add rest of batter and nuts. Bake 20 to 25 minutes. Cool and cut.

Brownies

4	eggs	2	squares unsweetened Bakers Chocolate
2	cup sugar	1	stick butter
1	cup flour	1	teaspoon vanilla
½	teaspoon salt	1	cup nuts (optional)

Mix eggs, sugar, flour and salt. Melt chocolate with butter in microwave. Pour over dry ingredients. Mix all together. Bake in 9 x 13-inch greased and floured pan, 350° for 25 minutes.

Penny Gressett

Praline Cookies

1¾	cups salted butter	1	teaspoon vanilla extract
1½	cups light brown sugar	¼	teaspoon salt
¼	cup sugar	1¼	cups chopped pecans
1	egg yolk	2	cups flour

Cream 1 cup butter, ¾ cup brown sugar and ¼ cup sugar in a mixer bowl until light and fluffy. Beat in the egg yolk, vanilla and salt. Stir in ½ cup pecans and the flour. Press into a greased 10 x 15-inch baking pan. Bake at 350° for 15 minutes. Combine the remaining ¾ cup butter and ¾ cup brown sugar in a saucepan. Bring to a boil over high heat. Cook for 3 minutes, stirring constantly. Remove the cookie dough from the oven. Prick holes over the surface with a fork. Pour the hot syrup over the dough, spreading over the surface. Bake for 3 to 5 minutes. Place on a wire rack. Sprinkle the remaining ¾ cup pecans over the top. Cool for 15 minutes. Cut into 1-inch squares. Cool completely before removing from the pan.

Chocolate Bits Raisin Squares

2 eggs	⅔ cup flour
⅔ cup sugar	½ teaspoon salt
⅔ cup seedless raisins	½ teaspoon baking powder
1 small package chocolate chips	4 tablespoons melted butter
1 teaspoon vanilla	

Beat eggs, adding gradually sugar, and the rest of the ingredients. Spread on well greased pan (9 x 9-inch or 9 x 13-inch). Bake 350° for 20 to 25 minutes. Let cool and sprinkle with powdered sugar. Then cut when cooled.

Ann Burney Eidschun Shotmeyer

Russian Fruit Cake Cookies

3 cups flour	½ teaspoon vanilla extract
½ teaspoon salt	1 teaspoon cinnamon
½ teaspoon baking powder	1 teaspoon ground cloves
3 eggs	1 teaspoon nutmeg
1 stick butter	2 pounds chopped dates
1¼ cups sugar	½ pound chopped pineapple
½ cup warm water	½ pound cherries
1 teaspoon lemon flavoring	4 cups pecans (not chopped)
½ teaspoon orange flavoring	½ teaspoon baking powder

Sift flour and salt over fruit and mix well. Cream butter and sugar. Add beaten eggs and baking powder. Add spices and flavorings with warm water and put in butter and sugar mixture. Pour all this over fruit and mix well. Drop teaspoon size on greased cookie sheet and bake at 350° for 15 minutes.

300 cookies

Julia Brown from Bea Chandler

Caramel Slice

Carol's favorite teatime office dessert.

¼ cup butter	¾ cup flour
1 cup brown sugar	1 teaspoon baking powder
1 egg	¼ teaspoon salt
½ cup chopped walnuts	1 cup flaked coconut

Melt butter in large saucepan. Remove from heat. Add sugar. Stir in beaten egg. Measure in nuts, flour, baking powder, salt, and coconut. Stir well. Scrape into greased 9 x 9-inch pan. Bake in 350° oven for 30 minutes. Frost when cool with Caramel Icing.

Caramel Icing:

¼ cup butter	2 tablespoons milk
½ cup brown sugar	1 cup powdered sugar

Combine butter, sugar, and milk in saucepan. Bring to boil and simmer 2 minutes. Cool. To speed up this procedure, run some cold water in the sink. Set pan in water. Stir until cool. Stir in sugar. If too stiff, add more milk until soft enough to spread. Smooth over bars. Cut when set.

Yield 36 bars

Jean Sorrels

Apricot Bars

1½ cups flour	1 cup brown sugar
1 teaspoon baking powder	¾ cup butter
¼ teaspoon salt	¾ cup apricot jam
1½ cups oats	

Mix dry ingredients with butter. Pat ⅔ of mixture into 11 x 7-inch pan. Spread jam over mixture. Add pecans. Sprinkle remaining mixture on top. Bake 375° for 35 minutes.

Almond Butter Bars

½ cup butter	½ cup firmly packed brown sugar
½ cup powdered sugar	1 tablespoon water
1 cup flour	¾ cup sliced almonds
3 tablespoons butter	½ teaspoon almond extract
¾ cup lemon juice	

Beat butter and powdered sugar until fluffy. Beat in flour. Press into ungreased 9-inch square pan. Bake at 350° for 12 to 15 minutes or until lightly browned. Remove from oven. In small saucepan, melt 3 tablespoons butter. Stir in lemon juice, brown sugar, and water. Bring to a boil, stirring constantly. Remove from heat. Stir in almonds and extract. Spread evenly over crust. Bake for 10 to 15 minutes or until it is bubbly in center. Cool slightly, then cut into bars.

Carol Sims

Helen's Lemon Squares

1 cup all-purpose flour	½ cup confectioners' sugar
½ cup butter	

Heat oven 350°. Mix thoroughly the above ingredients. Press into a square pan 8 x 8-inch building up ½-inch edge. Bake 20 minutes.

Mix and pour over crust:

2 eggs	½ teaspoon salt
1 cup granulated sugar	3 tablespoons fresh lemon juice
2 tablespoons flour	

Beat remaining ingredients until light and fluffy. Pour over hot crust. Bake again about 25 minutes or just until no imprint remains when lightly touched in center. Cool and sprinkle with confectioners' sugar. Cut into squares.

Makes 2 dozen

Helen Grant Maddox

Ryan's Lemon Iced Bars

½ cup butter
1 cup flour

¼ cup sugar

Mix well, press in 7 x 11-inch pan. Bake 15 minutes at 325°.

2 tablespoons flour
1 tablespoon lemon juice
2 beaten eggs

1 cup sugar
¼ teaspoon baking powder

Sift dry ingredients, add eggs, lemon juice and rind. Pour on baked crust. Bake 25 minutes at 350°. Cool. Spread lemon icing on top.

Lemon Icing:
2 tablespoons butter
¼ cup lemon juice

1 box confectioners' sugar
(¾ plastic bag)

Ryan Sims (my oldest son)

Peanut Butter Cookies

¾ cup creamy peanut butter
½ cup Crisco Shortening
1¼ cups firmly packed light brown sugar
3 tablespoons milk

1 tablespoon vanilla
1 egg
1¾ cups all-purpose flour
¾ teaspoon salt
¾ teaspoon baking soda

Heat oven to 375°. Combine peanut butter, shortening, light brown sugar, milk, and vanilla in large bowl. Beat at medium speed until well blended. Add egg. Beat just until blended. Combine flour, salt, and baking soda. Add to creamed mixture at low speed. Mix just until blended. Drop by heaping teaspoonfuls 2 inches apart onto ungreased baking sheet. Flatten slightly in crisscross pattern with fork. Bake for 7 to 8 minutes or until set and just beginning to brown.

Sunburst Lemon Squares

Crust:
2 cups all-purpose flour   1 cup butter
½ cup powdered sugar

Glaze:
1 cup powdered sugar   3 tablespoons fresh lemon juice

Filling:
4 eggs, slightly beaten   1 teaspoon baking powder
2 cups sugar   ¼ cup lemon juice
¼ cup flour

Heat oven to 350°. In large bowl, combine 2 cups flour, ½ cup powdered sugar and butter at low speed until crumbly. Press mixture evenly in bottom of ungreased 13 x 9-inch pan. Bake at 350° for 20 to 30 minutes or until light golden brown. In large bowl, combine eggs, sugar, ¾ cup flour and baking powder; blend well. Stir in lemon juice. Pour mixture over warm crust. Return to oven and bake 25 to 30 minutes or until top is light golden brown. Cool completely. Prepare glaze and drizzle over bars.

Karen Gintz

Connie's Peanut Butter Bars

1 cup sugar   6 cups Special K Cereal
1 cup corn syrup   2 cups butterscotch chips
1½ cups peanut butter (creamy)   1 cup chocolate chips
2 teaspoons vanilla

Bring corn syrup and sugar to boil and add peanut butter. Add vanilla. When smooth take off heat and add cereal. Press in 9 x 13-inch pan. Melt chocolate and butterscotch chips in microwave and spread over bars. Cool and cut into squares.

Connie Trautman

Yummy!

Candy & Desserts

Strawberries on a Cloud

This is one of my boys' favorite desserts. They often request this in place of a birthday cake. I usually have to make two.

Ingredients for Crust:

3 egg whites	¾ cup sugar
¼ teaspoon cream of tartar	

Ingredients for Filling:

1 (8-ounce) package cream cheese	1 large carton Light Cool Whip
1 cup sugar	3 cups fresh strawberries sliced
1 teaspoon vanilla	

This dessert is best made the day you are going to serve it and needs at least an hour in the refrigerator. Beat egg whites with cream of tartar until foamy. Add sugar a little at a time until stiff peaks form. Spread meringue on brown paper or pastry paper on cookie sheet to make a round crust with a well in the center. Bake at 275° for 1½ hours. Turn oven off, and leave in oven until it's cooled. (The crust can be made the day before.)

In a mixer, blend the cream cheese, sugar and vanilla until smooth. Fold in the cool whip and spread over the meringue shell. After slicing the strawberries, lightly sprinkle with powdered sugar to slightly sweeten them. Carefully place sliced strawberries on the top of the cream cheese mixture with larger, more beautiful slices on the top. Cool for 1 hour.

Carol Sims

Tea urges tranquility of the soul.

~Henry Wadsworth Longfellow

Southern English Toffee

3   cups pecans, slightly toasted or
    dried out in oven
1½ cups unsalted butter
    (no margarine)
1   pound milk chocolate candy
    melted (World's Finest Milk
    Chocolate)

2   cups white sugar
10 tablespoons cold water
½   teaspoon salt
1   tablespoon white corn syrup
1   teaspoon vanilla extract, optional

Grease the sides of a heavy saucepan (3-quart) with butter. Add water first; add butter, allow to melt on low heat, bring to a boil. Remove from heat. Add sugar, salt and corn syrup. (Corn syrup helps prevent sugaring of the candy.) Return to heat, stir until sugar is dissolved. Turn to medium high heat, stirring constantly with a long handle wooden spoon. Wash down sides of the saucepan with a pastry brush dipped in cold water (shake off any drops of water), thereby removing crystals, which cause the candy to sugar. Or being very careful, the saucepan can be partially covered for about two minutes to create steam to help wash down crystals. Cook to Hard Crack Stage which is 310°F or 154°C on a candy thermometer or "Mixture is very brittle when dropped into cold water and will not stick to teeth."

This is the critical stage. It takes approximately 20 minutes to cook to this stage. If not cooked long enough at medium high temperature, the sugar will not melt sufficiently, resulting in candy that is not brittle and will be sugary. If overcooked, it burns. When the hard crack stage is reached, add the coarser nuts and vanilla. Do as little stirring as possible after the nuts are added; can cause candy to sugar.

Pour into the greased pans. Let mixture run to sides and cover most of the pan, pushing with a metal spatula which has been greased with butter. Melt ½ pound of the milk chocolate candy in the top of a double boiler over simmering water (do not let the water boil). The chocolate can be melting on a back burner while the candy is being cooked. Using a spatula, spread the melted chocolate evenly over the top of the candy. Sprinkle generously with half of the finer ground pecans. Press the nuts down into the chocolate with a metal spatula. Cool a few minutes or until chocolate has nearly hardened. Score candy, marking 1¼-inch with a heavy knife. Do not cut all the way

Southern English Toffee continued

through the candy. Let cool until chocolate becomes firm. Turn candy upside down into the same jelly-roll pan or place a cookie sheet or another jelly roll pan on top of the candy and turn over. Spread the remaining milk chocolate (½ pound); sprinkle with the remaining finer ground nuts. When cold, break into 1 to 1¼-inch squares along the scored lines. Store in metal tins.

This recipe comes from Fay Brewer in Atlanta who taught Helen Maddox how to make it. It's wonderful!

Almond Bark Candy

Put a 2 pound package almond bark candy in a large pot in oven at 250° until it melts or melt in the microwave. Add these ingredients as follows:

1	(18-ounce) jar chunky peanut butter	1	(12-ounce) jar dry roasted peanuts
1	cup Rice Krispies	4	cups mini marshmallows

Mix together and place by teaspoonfuls onto waxed paper on a cookie sheet before it cools. Cool in refrigerator or freeze.

Marti's Mint Chocolate Candies

1	package starlight mints (crushed in blender or food processor)	2	tablespoons Crisco
1	package white chocolate morsels	¾	cup semisweet chocolate chips

Microwave white morsels with 1 tablespoon Crisco. Add crushed mint candy. Drop small candies on wax paper on a cookie sheet. Put in refrigerate. Microwave chocolate chips with 1 tablespoon Crisco. Dip hardened candies in chocolate.

Marti Greenman Steckbauer

Southern Pralines

(Microwave)

1½ cups firmly packed light brown sugar
⅔ cup half-and-half

⅛ teaspoon salt
2 tablespoons butter
1½ cups pecan halves

Combine sugar, half-and-half and salt in a deep 3-quart glass bowl. Mix well. Stir in butter. Microwave at HIGH for 7 to 9½ minutes or until mixture reaches soft boil stage (235°) stirring once. (In my microwave, it takes 11 minutes.) Beat by hand until mixture is creamy and begins to thicken (about 3 minutes). Add pecans. Drop by tablespoonfuls onto waxed paper; let stand until firm.

Yield: 2 dozen

Wonderful Fudge

1 stick butter
1 (12-ounce) can evaporated milk

4½ cups sugar (2 pounds)

In large pot over medium heat bring to boil about 5 to 7 minutes or until candy thermometer reaches 234° or less. Stir constantly to prevent scorching and remove from heat.

Add remaining ingredients in order given, stirring after each addition until well blended:

7 ounce jar marshmallow cream
1 ounce unsweetened chocolate
1 (12-ounce) package chocolate chips

3 bars German Chocolate (total 12 ounces Bakers)
1 tablespoon vanilla extract
Dash salt
1 cup pecans

Grease large jelly-roll pan (about 10 x 15½-inch). Pour and let cool and cut.

Makes 5 pounds

Helen Grant and Carol Maddox Forrester—Lauren Lewallen's favorite

Old-Fashioned Fudge

*My mother used to make fudge this way
and eat the whole thing herself. She loved chocolate!*

3	cups sugar	1½	cups milk
⅔	cup cocoa	¼	cup butter
⅛	teaspoon salt	1	teaspoon vanilla

Bring the sugar, cocoa, salt, and milk to a full boil in a heavy saucepan, stirring constantly. Once it reaches a boil, do not stir. Boil until it reaches 234°F on a candy thermometer to a softball stage in cold water. Remove from the heat and add butter and vanilla. Do not stir. Cool at room temperature to 110°F. Then beat with a wooden spoon until fudge thickens and loses some gloss. Quickly spread in a buttered 8 or 9-inch pan. Cut into squares and enjoy.

Ann Burney Eidschun Shotmeyer

Grandmommie's Chocolate/Macaroon Dessert

2	squares Bakers Unsweetened Chocolate	½	cup sugar
2	dozen almond macaroon cookies	1	envelope plain gelatin (unflavored)
2	cups milk	1	tablespoon vanilla
3	eggs (separate yolks and whites)	1	pint whipping cream or large Cool Whip

Make custard in double boiler (egg yolks, milk and sugar). Cook slowly until it starts to thicken, then remove from heat and set aside. Melt chocolate and add to custard. Break up cookies in small pieces and place in a large bowl. Dissolve gelatin in ¼ cup of cold water. Pour custard into large bowl with cookies. Add vanilla and gelatin. Beat egg whites until stiff and fold into custard mixture. Spray circular mold with Pam and pour custard mixture into mold. Refrigerate for 6 hours or more. Remove from mold onto silver tray to serve. Fill inside of mold with whipped cream or cool whip.

Helen Grant Maddox

This recipe was my husband's (Henry Maddox) grandmother's (Mrs. McDuffie) dessert. She served it on Christmas day for their large family gatherings. It has been a secret for over 30 years. I thought it was time to let others enjoy it.

Jonathan's Berry Crisp

¾ cup sugar
1 cup flour
½ cup butter

2 small cartons raspberries,
   blackberries, or blueberries

Preheat oven to 300°. For topping, mix together sugar and flour. Cut in ½ cup butter until mixture resembles cornmeal. Place berries in a small casserole dish. Spread topping firmly and evenly over berries. Bake 60 minutes. Let cool for 5 to 10 minutes uncovered. Serve with vanilla ice cream.

Jonathan Sims

Apple Peach Kuchen

Step 1:
1 cup margarine
½ cup flaked coconut

1 package yellow cake mix
½ cup chopped pecans

Cut margarine into cake mix until crumbly. Stir in coconut/nuts. Pat mixture into ungreased oblong pan building up slight edges. Bake 10 minutes at 350°.

Step 2:
1 cup sliced fresh apples or
   peaches

1 teaspoon cinnamon
½ cup sugar

Arrange apples on crust. Mix sugar and cinnamon together and sprinkle over apples.

Step 3:
1 cup sour cream

2 egg yokes or 1 egg

Blend together and drizzle over apples. Bake 25 minutes at 350°. Do not over bake.

Clifteen Samuelson

Fred's Bread Pudding

2	sticks butter	1	teaspoon vanilla
8	slices of day-old bread	1	cup raisins (light)
4	eggs	1	teaspoon fresh nutmeg
2	cups sugar	1	cup Meyers dark rum
2	cups milk		

Melt 2 sticks of butter in the microwave. Bake 8 slices of day-old bread with crust in 250° oven. Toast until crispy and break into bite-size pieces. Beat in mixer 4 eggs, 2 cups sugar, 2 cups milk, 1 teaspoon vanilla. Dip cut-up toast in butter, and place in casserole dish. Pour egg mixture over it. Press until absorbed. Spread 1 cup raisins (light) and 1 teaspoon nutmeg on top. Put in 400° oven for 1 hour. After 30 minutes of baking press down to get liquid to the top. Take out when firm, dark brown. Immediately after removing from the oven, pour 1 cup Meyers dark rum. Serve warm or cold.

Fred Craft—I usually ask Fred to make this for our family get-togethers. It's one of my favorite desserts.

Fluffy Tapioca Pudding

This old tapioca pudding recipe used to be on the Tapioca Pudding box, but the recipe was changed. I think this old recipe is the best way to prepare the pudding. I usually have to double this recipe every time I make it to have enough to last for the refrigerator. A favorite of my son Ben.

3	tablespoons Tapioca pudding	2	cups milk
3	tablespoons sugar	2	tablespoons sugar
1	egg yolk	1	egg white
⅓	teaspoon salt	¾	teaspoon vanilla

In saucepan mix pudding, 3 tablespoons sugar, egg yolk, salt, and milk. Heat slowly stirring constantly until pudding gets thick. While cooling the pudding, beat egg white until stiff, then add 2 tablespoons sugar and continue beating until stiff and glassy. Fold in egg white mixture into thick pudding, then add vanilla. This is delicious served warm or cold.

Carol Sims

Carol's Banana Pudding

2	eggs (separate egg whites)	1	teaspoon vanilla
2	cups milk	2-3	ripe bananas
1	cup sugar	1	box vanilla wafers
3	tablespoons flour		

Beat eggs. Mix flour and sugar and add to eggs. Add milk and slowly cook until thick. Beat egg whites until stiff; add 4 tablespoons sugar and beat until smooth and glassy. Arrange wafers and bananas in layers in a casserole dish. Pour pudding mixture over layers. Spread meringue on top. Brown meringue in oven at 425° for 2 minutes or until lightly brown.

Carol Sims

Easy Peach Cobbler

6-8	fresh peaches	5	slices of white bread
1½	cups sugar	1	egg
2	tablespoons flour	½	cup butter

Place peeled and cut-up peaches in 8-inch-square baking dish. Cut each slice of bread in 5 pieces and place over peaches. In a small bowl, combine sugar, flour, egg, and melted butter. Pour over bread. Bake 350° for 35 minutes or until brown.

Trifle

1	angel food cake (preferably Duncan Hines) cut up into big bite-size pieces		Vanilla pudding (made from scratch—use banana pudding recipe)
1	pint of fresh strawberries, raspberries, and blueberries	2	cups freshly whipped heavy whipping cream or Cool Whip Peach or Amaretto liqueur

Arrange in layers in a deep glass casserole or trifle dish the cake, pudding, berries and whipping cream sprinkling the liqueur along the way. Top with whipped cream and chocolate shavings and let sit in the refrigerator for 6 hours or overnight.

Carol Sims

Aussie Pavlova

6	egg whites at room temperature	1	teaspoon vinegar
1	cup sugar	1	tablespoon cornstarch
1	teaspoon vanilla		

First grease a flat tray (pizza or cookie sheet with no edge) and dust with flour or use parchment paper. Beat egg whites until they form peaks. Gradually beat in sugar, 1 teaspoon at a time until it dissolves. Fold in vinegar, vanilla, and cornstarch. Spread meringue onto baking tray, shaping into 8 to 10-inch circle with a well in the center. Bake in 200° to 220° oven for 2 hours or until outside is dry to touch. (An easy way to remove from the tray after it's cooled is to run dental floss underneath.) Fill the well with fresh fruit (bananas, kiwi, passion, strawberries, etc. and top with whipped cream.

Linda Sims—From my Aussie friend Fiona Emery.

Crème de Cacao Balls

2½	cups crushed chocolate sandwich cookies (Oreos)	⅓	cup crème de cacao
1	cup chopped walnuts	2	tablespoons dark corn syrup
1	cup sifted powdered sugar		Powdered sugar and cinnamon

Combine crushed cookies, walnuts, and 1 cup powdered sugar in large bowl. Add crème de cacao and corn syrup, mixing thoroughly. Shape mixture into 1-inch balls and roll each in powdered sugar. Place in an airtight container and chill overnight.

Yield: 3 dozen

Cakes

Julia's Sour Cream Pound Cake

We always look forward to Aunt Julia's pound cakes at Christmas!

½	pound butter (2 sticks)	3	cups flour
6	eggs	1	teaspoon baking powder
1½	teaspoons vanilla extract	1	pinch of salt
3	cups sugar	1	(8-ounce) carton sour cream

Cream butter and sugar until fluffy. Add eggs one at a time while beating. Sift flour, salt and baking powder. Add half to batter. Add sour cream, then remainder of flour. Bake at 325° in tube or Bundt pan (greased) for 1 hour 30 minutes. Important: you must not open the door at all during baking time and do not slam any doors in the house during that time.

Cream Cheese Pound Cake

Extraordinary, even when it doesn't cook enough! The first time I made this, it didn't cook enough in the center. Everyone thought I had made this wonderful crème brûlée pound cake.

1½	cups (3 sticks) butter	1	tablespoon vanilla extract
1	(8-ounce) package cream cheese	1	tablespoon almond extract
2⅔	cups sugar	3	cups cake flour
6	eggs	¼	teaspoon salt

Cream butter, cream cheese, and sugar. Add eggs one at a time. Add flavorings. Gradually beat in flour and salt, mixing well. Pour into greased and floured Bundt pan; bake at 300° for 1 hour, 15 minutes. Cool 10 minutes in pan.

Carol Sims

Carol's Pound Cake

1½ cups softened butter
3 cup sugar
8 eggs

3 cups all-purpose flour
6 tablespoons milk
1½ teaspoons vanilla

Cream butter and add sugar, beating until light and smooth. Add eggs and flour alternately, mixing well. Add milk and vanilla extract; mix until smooth. Pour batter into a greased and floured tube or Bundt pan. Place in a cold oven and turn heat to 325°. Bake for 1½ hours.

Carol Sims

Fred's Apple Dapple Cake

Delicious and addicting!

3 cups flour
1 teaspoon baking soda
1 teaspoon salt
1¼ cups oil
2 cups sugar

3 eggs
3 medium tart apples peeled and sliced
1 teaspoon vanilla

Mix dry ingredients. Mix oil and sugar. Beat eggs in one at a time. Put in flour mixture. Stir in apples. Put in greased Bundt pan. Bake 1 hour, 15 minutes at 350°.

Icing:

1 cup dark brown sugar
¼ cup milk

½ cup butter
1 teaspoon vanilla

Five minutes before cake is finished combine ingredients over low heat until melted. Boil for 3 minutes or until it coats the spoon. When cake is finished, put cake on rack with a pan under it and drizzle icing over cake. Continue to drizzle icing that falls into pan over cake by moving rack over another pan while scraping icing. You will probably have to do this about 4 to 5 times until icing is used up. Don't spread icing with a spatula, just drizzle.

Fred Craft

Dried Apple Cake

1	pound dried apples chopped, washed, and drained	4	eggs
2	cups dark syrup	1	pound raisins
1	cup butter	2	cups pecans
1¼	cups sugar	1	teaspoon cake spice
3	cups flour	1	teaspoon baking soda
		2	teaspoons baking powder

Caramelize apples in dark syrup for 1 hour. Cool. Mix well. Bake 2 hours at 250° in Bundt pan.

Donna Schroeder

Caramel Secrets

As the sugar melts, the color progresses from pale yellow to brown. Use a large cast-iron skillet or heavy saucepan to achieve even browning. For best results use a wooden spoon, it can take the heat and the handle doesn't get hot.

• Cook over medium-high heat until the sugar turns a rich caramel color. Carefully pour the caramelized sugar into the whipping cream. Use a large pot, because the mixture bubbles as the cream and sugar combine.

• There's no guesswork when you use a thermometer that signals when proper temperature is reached.

• Cleanup is a snap when you soak the utensils in hot water to remove all hardened caramel.

Tip: You can make caramel sauce on a humid day, but save cake frostings for a clear, dry day.

Buttermilk Layer Cake

1	cup shortening	½	teaspoon salt
2	cups sugar	½	teaspoon baking soda
3	large eggs	1½	cups buttermilk
2½	cups all-purpose flour	2	teaspoons vanilla extract

Beat shortening at medium speed with an electric mixer until creamy. Gradually add sugar, beating well. Add eggs, one at a time, beating until blended after each addition. Combine flour, salt, and soda; add to shortening mixture alternately with buttermilk, beginning and ending with flour mixture. Beat at low speed until blended after each addition. Beat at medium-high speed 2 minutes. Stir in vanilla. Pour batter into 3 greased and floured 8-inch round cake pans. Bake at 350° for 22 minutes or until a wooden pick inserted in center comes out clean. Cool in pans on wire racks 10 minutes; remove from pans. Cool completely on wire racks. Spread Caramel Frosting (recipe follows) between layers and on top and sides of cake.

Helen Foster

Caramel Frosting

3¾ cups sugar	¼	cup butter
1½ cups whipping cream	¼	teaspoon baking soda

Bring 3 cups sugar, cream, butter, and baking soda to a boil in a heavy saucepan. Remove from heat, and keep warm. Sprinkle remaining ¾ cup sugar in a heavy saucepan. Cook over medium heat, stirring constantly, until sugar melts and syrup is light golden brown. (Sugar will clump before melting.) Gradually pour into whipping cream mixture. (Mixture will bubble.) Stir until smooth. Cook over medium heat, stirring often, 10 to 12 minutes or until a candy thermometer registers 240° (softball stage). Remove from heat. Beat at high speed with an electric mixer until spreading consistency (8 to 10 minutes).

Yields 3 cups

Carol Sims—from Helen Foster, a caramel lover like myself.

Coconut Layer Cake

Cake:

2	sticks softened unsalted butter
2	cups sugar
4	large eggs at room temperature
1½	cups self-rising flour

1¼	cups all-purpose flour
1	cup milk
1	teaspoon vanilla extract

Filling:

1	cup milk
½	cup sugar
2	tablespoons all-purpose flour

1	(7-ounce) package sweetened shredded coconut
1	teaspoon vanilla extract

Frosting:

3	large egg whites
1½	teaspoons vanilla extract
½	cup cold water

1½	cups sugar
⅜	teaspoon cream of tartar (equals ¼ plus ⅛ teaspoon)

Preheat oven to 350°. Grease 3 (9 x 2-inch) cake pans, spray pans with Baker's Joy. Set aside. To make the cake, in a large bowl with an electric mixer cream the butter, add the sugar, a little at a time, and beat the mixture until light and fluffy. Add the eggs, one at a time, beating well after each addition. Combine the flours and add to the butter mixture in four parts, alternating with the milk and the vanilla extract, beating well after each addition. (For a variation, you could use almond extract instead of vanilla.) Divide the batter among the cake pans. Bake for 20 to 25 minutes, or until a cake tester inserted into the centers of cakes comes out clean. Let cakes cool in pans for 10 minutes. Invert onto racks and let cool. To make the filling, in a saucepan combine the milk, sugar, and flour and whisk mixture until smooth. Cook over moderately high heat, whisking constantly, for 5 minutes, or until thickened and bubbly. Remove from heat and add the coconut, reserving a handful. Stir in the vanilla extract. Cover and cook to room temperature. (Another variation for the filling is ½ cup coconut, ¾ milk, ½ cup sugar, 2 tablespoons flour, ¼ cup chopped toasted almonds, ¼ cup maraschino cherries, 1 teaspoon almond extract—this filling is best when you use the almond extract in the cake mix.)

Assemble the cake when it is cool, spreading the filling between the layers and ready to be iced before you make the icing.

Coconut Layer Cake continued

To make the frosting: In a large bowl with an electric mixer combine the egg whites and the vanilla extract. In a saucepan over moderately high heat combine the water with the sugar and cream of tartar. As mixture begins to bubble at edges, stir once to make sure the sugar is dissolved completely, then let it come to a rolling boil (about 2 to 3 minutes). Remove immediately from heat. With the electric mixer on medium-high, beat the whites and the vanilla extract until foamy, about 1 minute. Without turning off the mixer, pour the sugar syrup into the beaten egg whites in a thin, steady stream. Continue beating constantly, on medium high speed, for about 5 minutes or until stiff peaks form but frosting is still creamy. Frost tops and sides of cake immediately and sprinkle top with reserved coconut.

Ginny's 1-2-3-4 Layer Cake

4	eggs (separate yolks and egg whites)	1	cup milk
2	sticks margarine	3	teaspoons baking powder
3	cups flour	½	teaspoon salt
2	cups sugar	1	teaspoon almond extract

Cream sugar and margarine 10 minutes with mixer. Add egg yolks one at a time. Add ⅓ of flour mixture (with baking powder and salt) before adding milk. Add flavoring before adding last of flour. Fold in beaten egg whites. Pour batter in greased and floured cake pans (3) at 350° for 20 minutes. Ice with 7-Minute Icing or Caramel Icing.

Ginny Sims Craft

The secret to cake making is to add flour first and flour last mixed with milk.

Angel Food Cake

1¼ cups sifted cake flour
½ cup sifted sugar
1½ cups egg whites (12 large eggs) at room temperature
¼ teaspoon salt

1¼ teaspoons cream of tartar
1 teaspoon vanilla extract
1 teaspoon almond extract
1⅓ cups sifted sugar

Preheat oven to 375°. Sift flour and ½ cup sugar together four times. Set aside. Combine egg whites, salt, cream of tartar, and flavorings in a large bowl. Beat with an electric mixer until moist, soft peaks form. Add remaining sugar in four additions, beating until blended each time. By hand, carefully fold flour/sugar mixture into egg whites in four additions until all is incorporated. Pour batter into an ungreased 10-inch tube pan. Bake for 35 to 40 minutes. Remove from oven and invert cake so that pan rests on protruding center tube or side extensions. If pan has neither, place the tube over a bottle. Cool about 1½ hours. Loosen sides of the cake with a thin-bladed knife, and remove from pan.

My favorite cake has always been Angel Food. As a child, when I would visit my Grandmother Burney, after arriving at her home, I would sneak into the kitchen to see if she had made me an angel food cake (her specialty) which she would always keep on top of the refrigerator in her Tupperware caketaker. Unfortunately, I do not have her recipe, but I do have very sweet memories.

My son, eat honey because it is good, and the honeycomb which is sweet to your taste; So shall the knowledge of wisdom be to your soul.

~Psalms 24:13-14

Carrot Cake

2	cups flour	1	cup canola oil
2	teaspoons baking powder	2	cups brown sugar
1½	teaspoons cinnamon	4	eggs
2	teaspoons baking soda	1	cup chopped nuts
½	teaspoon salt	3	cups grated carrots

Mix dry ingredients; add oil and blend. Add eggs one at a time and beat after each addition. Add carrots and nuts and blend well. Bake in 2 round (9-inch) pans or 1 (9 x 13-inch) pan at 350° for 30 minutes (45 minutes if in one big pan).

Cream Cheese Frosting

1	(8-ounce) package cream cheese	1	pound box powdered sugar
½	cup butter	2	teaspoons vanilla extract

Mix together in electric mixer until smooth and ice the cake putting icing between layers.

Praline Cheesecake

1	cup graham cracker crumbs	2	tablespoons flour
3	tablespoons sugar	3	eggs
4	tablespoons butter	1½	teaspoons vanilla
3	(8-ounce) packages cream cheese	½	cup finely chopped pecans
1½	cups packed brown sugar		

Combine crumbs, sugar, butter and press into bottom of 9-inch springform pan. Bake at 350° for 10 minutes. Combine cream cheese, brown sugar, and flour; beat at medium speed in mixer until well blended. Add eggs, one at a time, mixing well after each addition. Blend in vanilla and pecans. Pour over crumbs; bake at 350° for 55 minutes. Loosen from rim of pan. Cool and chill. Ice with maple syrup, brushing over rim with pecan halves.

Jennifer's Mississippi Cheesecake

Prepare cookie crust first:

1 cup flour	1 egg yolk, slightly beaten
¼ cup sugar	¼ teaspoon vanilla
½ cup butter	

Mix flour and sugar. Cut in butter until crumbly, then add egg yolk and vanilla and blend thoroughly. Pat ⅓ of dough on bottom of 9-inch springform pan with sides removed. Bake in hot oven at 400° for 6 minutes or until golden brown, cool.

Butter sides of pan and attach to bottom. Pat remaining dough evenly on sides to a height of 2 inches.

Filling:

2 (8-ounce) package cream cheese	2 teaspoons vanilla
1 cup sugar	½ teaspoon almond extract
3 eggs	3 cups sour cream

Prepare above ingredients at room temperature. Beat cream cheese and sugar. Add eggs, vanilla and almond extract. Beat until smooth. Blend in sour cream by hand. Pour into prepared crust and bake at 375° for 55 minutes. Turn off oven and allow cake to remain in oven for 1 hour more. Chill well after allowing cake to cool out of the oven.

Jennifer Bailey Locke

Thank God for tea! What would the world do without tea?
How did it exist? I am glad I was not born before tea.

~Rev. Sydney Smith,
Lady Holland's Memoir

Pumpkin Cheesecake

16 ounces cream cheese
16 ounces can pumpkin
¾ cup sugar

½ teaspoon each—nutmeg, ginger, cinnamon
¼ teaspoon salt
2 eggs

Beat up cheese and spices (not pumpkin) until light and fluffy. Add pumpkin, eggs—beat one at a time. Pour into graham cracker crust in springform pan. Bake for 50 minutes 350°.

Topping:
16 ounces sour cream
¾ teaspoon vanilla

¼ cup sugar

Combine sour cream with vanilla. Add sugar and stir.

Sherry Cream Angel Food Cake

Make the Duncan Hines angel food cake mix or from scratch and then ice.

Icing for angel food cake:
4 egg yolks
½ cup Sherry
½ cup sugar

1 tablespoon gelatin softened in ¼ cup cold water

Cook egg yolks, sherry, and sugar in double broiler until thickens, stirring constantly. Add gelatin and stir until dissolved. Cool. Beat 4 egg whites and ½ cup sugar until stiff. Whip well ½ pint heavy cream. Fold yolk mixture into cream, then fold in whites. Cut angel food cake into 3 layers and spread with icing.

Tipsy Cake

Traditional Williamsburg Recipe

Take two layers of sponge cake and soak them well in Sherry and chill well. Take a quart of boiled custard and pour part of it over one layer. Add the second layer and sprinkle with sliced blanched almonds. Pour the remaining custard over it. Cover the top with whipping cream and a few chopped toasted almonds.

Julia Brown

Old-Fashioned Light Fruit Cake

*It took me many years to get this wonderful recipe
from Aunt Julia. She used to send us this cake every year at Christmas.
It's better than any fruit cake I've ever had!*

4	cups pecans (do not chop)	1	ounce bottle Frenchee's Brandy flavoring
1	pound candied cherries		
2	pounds mixed candied fruit	4	cups sifted flour
1	pound seedless white raisins	1	teaspoon nutmeg
½	pound soft butter	1½	teaspoons cinnamon
2¼	cups sugar	1	teaspoon salt
6	eggs		

Mix butter, sugar, eggs, and flavoring in a large bowl with an electric mixer. Sift together dry ingredients. Add this to the butter and egg mixture. Add fruit and nuts with a heavy spoon. Fill pans (sprayed generously with Baker's Joy or lined with foil) ⅔ full. For loaves, bake at 275° for 2 hours. For tube pan, bake at 275° for 3 hours. When cake is half cooked, brush top with honey or light corn syrup. Decorate with nuts and fruit. Press them down into the cake to make them stick. Then return back to the oven to finish cooking. After the cake cools, peel off foil and keep in a tin covered with wine soaked cheese cloth. Keep stored in tight container for 3 weeks before serving. If necessary resoak cheese cloth.

Save some of the candied fruit to decorate. Use 2 loaf pans or one tube pan lined with foil or greased well with Baker's Joy.

Julia Brown

Coconut-Sour Cream Layer Cake

1   butter flavored cake mix
2   cups sugar
1   (16-ounce) carton sour cream

1   (12-ounce) frozen coconut
    thawed

Prepare cake mix according to package directions, making two 8-inch layers; when completely cool, split both layers. Combine sugar, sour cream, and coconut, blending well; chill. Reserve 1 cup of sour cream mixture for frosting. Spread remainder between layers of cake. Combine reserved sour cream mixture with whipped topping; blend until smooth. Spread on top and sides of cake. Store cake in an airtight container and refrigerate for 3 days before serving.

DeeDee Sims (Thomasville, Georgia)

Poppy Seed Cake

2   cups flour
1   cup margarine (2 sticks)

3   tablespoons sugar
½   cup chopped walnuts

Blend these together and press into a 9 x 13-inch pan. Bake at 375° for 20 minutes.

Cook the following to make a custard:
1½ cups milk
4   egg yolks
½   teaspoon salt

2   heaping teaspoons cornstarch
1   cup sugar

After cooking custard, dissolve 1 package unflavored gelatin in ¼ cup cool water. Add to custard and then add ¼ cup poppy seeds. Beat 4 egg whites until stiff and gradually add ½ cup sugar and 1 teaspoon cream of tartar. Fold mixture into the custard. Pour over the crust. Refrigerate and top with whipped cream and nuts.

Linda Sims

Jael McClure gave me this recipe—it is really good!

Red Velvet Cake

Grease and flour 2 (9-inch) layer pans.

1½ cups sugar	1 teaspoon vanilla
½ cup butter	1 cup buttermilk
2 eggs	2½ cups cake four
2 tablespoons cocoa	1½ teaspoons baking soda
2 ounces red food coloring	1 tablespoon vinegar
1 teaspoon salt	

Cream butter, sugar, and eggs very well. Make a paste of the cocoa and food coloring. Then add to the creamed mixture. Mix the salt, vanilla, and buttermilk. Add this alternately with the flour to the mixture. Mix the baking soda and vinegar together, then fold into the batter. Do not beat. Bake in preheated oven 350° for 30 minutes.

Icing:

5 teaspoons flour	1 cup butter
1 cup milk	1 teaspoon vanilla
1 cup granulated sugar	

Cook flour and milk over medium heat until thick, stirring constantly. Set aside until cool. Beat butter, sugar, and vanilla until creamed well. Beat both mixtures together and put on cake.

Carol Sims

A Teatime Blessing—
Lord, grant that our time together be steeped in serenity,
sweetened by sharing, and surrounded by the warm
fragrance of Your love. Amen

~Emilie Barnes,
If Teapots Could Talk

Mimi's Breaky Icing Cake

2 cups sugar
1 cup shortening
   Dash of salt
1 teaspoon vanilla
4 eggs (Cream well adding eggs
   one at a time.)
1 cup buttermilk with 1 teaspoon
   baking soda dissolved in it

2½ cups sifted flour
   Alternate milk and flour.
1 bar German chocolate melted in ½
   cup hot water OR 2 tablespoons
   cocoa, 1 tablespoon sugar, ½ cup
   hot water

Mix together. Bake 350° in 3 (9 or 8-inch) cake pans (greased and floured) for 30 to 35 minutes.

Chocolate Fudge Icing

Scald: ⅔ cup milk

Add:

2 squares (2 ounces) unsweetened
   chocolate (cut into pieces) OR
   2 tablespoons cocoa

2 cups sugar
2 tablespoons light corn syrup
⅛ teaspoon salt

Cook slowly, stirring until sugar dissolves. Cook to soft ball stage (238°F). Test by dropping a few drops in a cup of cold water.

Remove from heat and add 2 tablespoons butter. Cool to lukewarm (110°F) without stirring. Add 1 teaspoon vanilla. Beat until icing thickens a little and quickly ice cake.

Jennifer Rayford Sims

This is my grandmother Mimi's (Zelma McKenzie) famous chocolate cake recipe.

Aunt Julia's German Sweet Chocolate Cake

1	package (4 ounces) Baker's German Sweet Chocolate	1	teaspoon vanilla
½	cup boiling water	1½	cups sifted flour
1	cup butter	1	teaspoon baking soda
2	cups sugar	½	teaspoon salt
4	egg yolks	1	cup buttermilk
		4	egg whites stiffly beaten

Melt chocolate in boiling water and cool. Cream butter and sugar until fluffy. Add egg yokes one at a time beating well after each egg. Blend in vanilla and chocolate. Sift flour with soda and salt. Add dry mixture alternately with buttermilk to chocolate mixture, beating after each addition until smooth. Fold in beaten egg whites. Pour into 3 (9-inch) layer pans lined with wax paper. Bake 350° for 30 to 35 minutes.

Coconut Pecan Frosting

Combine 1 cup evaporated milk with 1 cup sugar, 3 slightly beaten egg yolks, ½ cup butter and 1 teaspoon vanilla. Cook and stir over medium heat until thickened (about 10 minutes). Add 1 can of angel flake coconut, 1 cup chopped nuts (pecans). Spread between layers and on sides.

Julia Brown

Celebrate the happiness that friends are always giving, making every day a holiday and celebrate just living.

~Amanda Bradley

Hershey's Perfectly Chocolate Cake

A man pleaser!

2 cups sugar
1¾ cups all-purpose flour
¾ cup Hershey Cocoa
1½ teaspoons baking powder
1½ teaspoons baking soda
1 teaspoon salt

2 eggs
1 cup milk
½ cup vegetable oil
2 teaspoons vanilla extract
1 cup boiling water

To intensify the flavor, I occasionally add a teaspoon of instant coffee to the cake batter.

Combine dry ingredients in a large bowl. Add eggs, milk, oil, and vanilla. Beat at medium speed for 2 minutes. Stir in boiling water (batter will be thin). Pour into greased and floured 9-inch round baking pans. Bake in 350° for 30 to 35 minutes or until toothpick comes out clean. Cool 10 minutes and remove to wire racks. Cool completely and frost.

Linda Sims

Perfectly Chocolate Frosting

1 stick butter
1 teaspoon vanilla
⅔ cup Hershey Cocoa

3 cups powdered sugar
⅓ cup milk

Melt butter. Stir in cocoa and add powdered sugar and milk, beating at medium speed until it reaches spreading consistency. Add more milk if needed. Stir in vanilla.

Makes about 2 cups

Mississippi Mud Cake

3	sticks butter		Dash of salt
½	cup cocoa	1	small package miniature
4	eggs		marshmallows
1½	cups flour	2	cups sugar
1½	cups pecans, chopped		

Melt butter; add cocoa with beaten eggs, then flour. Add flour, salt, and sugar. Beat well. Then add nuts. Pour in greased pan (13 x 9 x 2-inch) Bake for 35 minutes at 350°. Pour marshmallows over cake while hot. Put cake in warm oven until marshmallows melt.

Icing:

1	package powdered sugar	⅓	cup cocoa
½	stick soft butter or margarine	½	cup milk
½	teaspoon vanilla		

Mix ingredients, beat well. Pour over marshmallows. When cake cools, cut into squares.

Serves 20

Julia Brown

Pumpkin Cake

2	cups flour	½	teaspoon salt
2	cups sugar	½	teaspoon ground cloves
2	teaspoons baking powder	1	cup canola oil
1	teaspoon baking soda	1	(15-ounce) can pumpkin puree
1	teaspoon cinnamon	4	eggs
1	teaspoon nutmeg	½	cup nuts

Mix all dry ingredients. Then add wet. EASY! Poor batter in greased Bundt pan. Cook 35 to 40 minutes at 350°. Cool 10 minutes before turning cake over.

Carol Sims

Chocolate Cinnamon Sheet Cake

2	cups sugar	4	tablespoons cocoa
1	teaspoon soda	1	cup water
2	cups flour	½	cup buttermilk
1	teaspoon cinnamon	2	eggs
1	cup margarine	1	teaspoon vanilla

Blend sugar, soda, flour, and cinnamon in a large bowl. In a saucepan, melt margarine, cocoa and water. Bring to a boil and pour over dry mixture. Add buttermilk, eggs, and vanilla; mix well. Pour into a greased sheet pan. Bake for 20 minutes at 400°. Begin icing when cake is almost done.

Icing:

½	cup butter	1	box powdered sugar (3 cups)
4	tablespoons cocoa	1	teaspoon vanilla
6	tablespoons milk	1	cup chopped pecans

Melt butter with cocoa and milk. Bring to boil, then remove from heat. Stir in almost all of the box of powder sugar. Add vanilla and chopped pecans. Beat well and spread on hot cake.

Hershey Bar Cake

2	sticks margarine or butter	½	teaspoon baking soda
2	cups sugar	¼	teaspoon salt
4	eggs, well-beaten	1	cup buttermilk
1	(5½-ounce) can Hershey's syrup	2	teaspoons vanilla
2½ cups flour		7	small Hershey bars, melted

Cream butter and sugar. Add eggs and chocolate syrup. In separate bowl, sift together flour, soda, and salt. Add flour mixture alternately with buttermilk to chocolate mixture. Add vanilla and melted candy bars. Pour in greased and floured Bundt pan and bake at 350° for 1 hour.

Carol Sims

One of my son Ryan's favorites. Will stay moist for at least 7 days if you can keep it that long!

Pies

I usually use the Pillsbury pie crust in the red box in the refrigerator section of the grocery store, but here are other very good recipes.

Pie Crust Recipes

Mix together in KitchenAid or food processor:

1 teaspoon salt	4⅓ sticks Crisco
1 cup water	8¼ cups flour

Makes about 6 to 7 balls of dough. Cool before using. Can freeze.

OR

1 cup all-purpose flour	⅓ cup shortening
½ teaspoon salt	3 tablespoons cold water

Mix in the same way and chill before rolling into pie crust. Bake at 450° for 12 minutes for precooked pie shells.

Toll House Pie

2 eggs	1 cup chocolate chips
½ cup flour	(use butterscotch morsels
½ cup sugar	for a different taste)
½ cup brown sugar	1 cup chopped pecans
1 cup melted butter	

Mix all ingredients together. Pour into unbaked pie shell and bake at 325° for 1 hour or 55 minutes.

Carol Sims

Sugarless Apple Pie

Peel, core and slice apples into a deep dish pie shell. Melt one small can frozen Tree Top apple juice and ¾ stick butter. Boil; add cinnamon to taste. Place 2 to 3 tablespoons cornstarch in a cup of cold water Add to apple juice mixture to thicken. Pour on top of apples. Put another pastry on top. Bake at 325° for 20 minutes and at 200° for 1 hour.

Carol Sims

Streusel Pumpkin Pie

My family's favorite pumpkin pie.
People who don't like pumpkin pie usually like this one.

1½	cups canned pumpkin	¼	teaspoon cloves
¾	cup sugar	4	slightly beaten eggs
½	teaspoon salt	1	cup milk
1	teaspoon cinnamon	¾	cup evaporated milk
½	teaspoon ginger	1	(9-inch) pie shell
¼	teaspoon nutmeg		

Combine pumpkin, sugar, salt, and spices. Blend in eggs, milk, and evaporated milk. Pour into unbaked pie shell (not entirely full). Place in freezer for three hours. Right before baking, add streusel topping (recipe below) and bake.

Streusel Topping:

⅓	cup flour	3	tablespoons grated orange rind
⅓	cup firmly packed brown sugar	½	cup chopped pecans
3	tablespoons butter		

Combine flour and brown sugar in small bowl. Cut in butter until crumbly. Add orange rind and pecans. Mix well. Sprinkle mixture over top of frozen pie. Bake at 400° for about 1 hour, 15 minutes. Let cool before cutting. Serve with whipped cream (flavored with powdered sugar and brandy flavoring).

Carol Sims

Apple Caramel Crunch Pie

Our family thinks this is the best apple pie ever.
It's always on our Thanksgiving and Christmas menu!

1 (9-inch) deep dish pie shell uncooked

Filling:

3 tablespoons sugar
3 tablespoons flour
3 tablespoons lemon juice, freshly squeezed

5-6 Golden Delicious or Granny Smith apples peeled and thinly sliced (Granny Smith take longer to cook.)
⅓ cup milk

Dry Topping:

1 cup crushed graham crackers
½ cup sugar
¼ cup flour

1 teaspoon cinnamon
½ cup butter, melted
1 cup chopped pecans

Caramel Topping:

5 caramels
1 tablespoon butter

1½ teaspoons water

Preheat oven to 350°. Prepare the filling: in a small mixing bowl, combine sugar, flour, and lemon juice. Dredge apple slices in sugar mixture. Fill pie shell with apple slices. Pour milk over apples. Prepare dry topping: in a small mixing bowl, combine graham crumbs, sugar, flour, and cinnamon. Add melted butter to mixture. Completely cover apples with crumb mixture. Prepare Caramel topping: Place caramels, butter, and water in a very small microwave-safe container and microwave on medium-low heat until softened. Cool slightly so caramel mixture will not run off pie. Drizzle caramel mixture over top of pie. Bake 45-55 minutes or until apples soften, crust browns, and topping crisps.

Carol Sims

Aunt Julia's Pecan Pie

1	cup Karo syrup	1	teaspoon vanilla
½	cup sugar	1	cup pecan halves
3	eggs	½	teaspoon salt

Beat eggs slightly, add sugar, syrup, and nuts, salt, and vanilla. Put in unbaked pie shell and bake 350° for 50 minutes. The pecans will float to the top forming a crust.

Julia Brown

Jimmy's Caramel Pie

¾	cup sugar	3	tablespoons flour
2	cups milk	2	tablespoons butter
3	egg yolks	1	teaspoon vanilla
¼	cup sugar		

Prepare pie crust and bake. For filling, caramelize sugar by putting ¾ cup sugar into heavy sauce pan, and melt down completely, stirring as it melts so it will not burn. In a separate bowl, mix milk, egg yolks, ¼ cup sugar, and flour. Mix well with a whisk. When the caramelized sugar is a nice golden brown, pour the liquid in the sauce pan. It will bubble up and get hard like candy. Then patiently stir all of this over medium heat until all of the caramelized sugar has melted into the liquid. Stir until thickened and remove from heat. Add butter and vanilla. Pour into baked crust. Beat egg whites until stiff; add 4 tablespoons sugar, beating until smooth and glassy. Spread meringue on top. Brown meringue in oven at 425° for 2 minutes or until lightly brown.

Penny Gressett—Jimmy's favorite pie!

Connie's Pecan Pie

2	eggs	1	uncooked pie shell
1½	cups pecan halves cut up	1	cup light Karo syrup
2	tablespoons butter	1	teaspoon vanilla extract
½	cup sugar		Dash salt

Combine sugar, corn syrup, salt, and melted butter. Beat in eggs, add vanilla and pecans. Pour into pie shell. Cook 350° for 55 minutes.

Connie Goodson—my cousin from Atlanta, Georgia

Ann's Lemon Angel Pie

My mother's best dessert!

4	eggs separated		Juice and zest of 1 lemon
½	teaspoon cream of tartar	¼	cup water
1½	cups sugar	1	cup heavy cream, whipped

Beat egg whites until frothy and add cream of tartar. Beat until stiff. Add 1 cup of sugar gradually, beating constantly until glassy. Line bottom of a 9-inch pie plate with meringue. Bake in a very slow 275° oven for 1 hour.

Beat egg yolks in a double boiler until thick and light. Add remaining ½ cup sugar, lemon juice, rind, and ¼ cup water. Cook over hot water stirring constantly, until thick; cool. Let the meringue shell cool. Spread lemon filling on the bottom of the shell and then top with whipped cream. Store in the fridge.

This pie is also delicious made with chocolate. Melt 1 bar of Sweetened German Chocolate with 3 tablespoons water over low heat. Add 1 teaspoon vanilla. When cooled, fold 1 cup of whipping cream (real, not Cool Whip) into mixture. Put this mixture into meringue crust and chill. If you serve both of these at the same time, your guests will want a piece of each.

Ann Eidschun Shotmeyer

Easy Lemon Pie

1   can Eagle Brand Milk
1   small can frozen lemonade (thawed)

1   small carton Cool Whip

Mix all ingredients together and pour into a baked pie shell or a graham cracker crust. Do not cook mixture. Chill.

Key Lime Pie

Crust:

1   cup graham cracker crumbs
3   tablespoons sugar

4-5 tablespoons melted butter

Preheat oven to 325°. Crush graham crackers between two sheets of Saran wrap with a rolling pin or use the food processor. Mix graham cracker crumbs with sugar and melted butter. Press into 9-inch pie plate and bake for 5 minutes. Remove from and oven and let cool.

Filling:

½   cup fresh key lime juice
      (or ¼ cup key lime juice and
      ¼ cup lemon juice)
3   eggs
    Pinch cream of tartar

1   (14-ounce) can sweetened
      condensed milk
1   cup whipping cream
1   lime

Separate 2 of the eggs, placing the two egg whites into a mixing bowl. Reserve the yolks in another bowl. To the yolks, add one whole egg, ⅓ cup lime juice and sweetened condensed milk. Mix well. With clean mixer blades, beat the egg whites until stiff, not dry, adding salt and cream of tartar after about 20 seconds. Fold whites into filling mixture. Pour filling into partially baked crust. Bake 10 to 15 minutes at 350° or until set. Let cool at room temperature, then freeze for four hours. Just before serving, whip cream (adding 2 tablespoons powdered sugar). You may serve with a dollop of whip cream and a slice of lime or you may cover pie with whipped cream with pastry bag. If there is any left, store in the refrigerator.

Carol Sims—One of my husband Bob's favorites.

Sims Cream Cheese Peach Pie

*This is the Sims specialty in June and July when
the peaches are in season. There's never any leftover!*

1	baked pastry shell	1	cup sugar
1	(4-ounce) package cream cheese softened	¼	cup water
		2	tablespoons cornstarch
7	fresh peaches, sliced without skin (about 4 cups sprinkled with fruit fresh)	1	teaspoon almond flavoring
		1	small carton of Cool Whip or 8 ounces whipped cream

Soften the cream cheese and spread over pastry shell. Place 5 sliced peaches or enough peaches to fill pastry shell. Combine the sugar, water, cornstarch and remaining sliced peaches (1 cup) in a saucepan and cook, stirring until thickened. The thicker this sauce gets, the better. Cool and add almond flavoring. Pour sauce over peaches in the pastry shell and chill. Top with whip cream and serve.

Carol Sims

Ice Cream Pie

7	tablespoons melted butter	3	cups cornflakes
¼	cup brown sugar	⅓	cup finely chopped pecans
2	ounces unsweetened baking chocolate	1½	quarts ice cream (vanilla Haagen-Dazs—Mint Chip at Christmas)
½	cup semi-sweet chocolate chips		

In medium saucepan, melt butter, brown sugar, unsweetened chocolate and chocolate chips over low heat. Stir constantly until thoroughly mixed and sugar is dissolved. Place cornflakes and nuts in large bowl. Pour warm chocolate mixture over the corn flakes, gently stirring until flakes are thoroughly coated. Spray 9-inch plate with vegetable coating. Gently press coated flakes evenly into pie plate. Place in freezer until firm. Fill frozen chocolate shell with slightly softened ice cream. Freeze until firm. Top with Fudge Sauce, pg. 149, Praline Sauce, pg. 148, or berries.

Anderson Hotel Peach Pie

Prepare graham cracker crust or cookie crumb crust.

Graham cracker crust:
1½ cups graham crumbs ⅓ cup brown sugar
⅓ cup melted butter

Combine ingredients and press into pie plate. Bake at 375° for 4 minutes.

Cookie crumb crust:
½ cup melted butter ¼ cup sugar
1 cup flour

Mix well and press in pan. Bake 15 minutes 325°.

Filling:
Cream together 2 cups powdered sugar and ½ cup butter. Mix in 2 egg yolks and fold in 2 stiffly-beaten egg whites. Pour mixture into pie shell. Spread 4 to 6 freshly sliced peaches on top. Cover with whip cream. Chill.

Connie Trautman

Delicious! From the Anderson Hotel in the Midwest.

Strawberry Pie

1½ cups sugar Pinch salt
1½ cups water 1 small package strawberry jello
¼ cup cornstarch Cool Whip for garnish

Prepare pie shell and cool. Cook sugar, water, and cornstarch until smooth and clear. Remove from heat and add jello while hot. After mixture cools add fresh sliced strawberries to mixture and place in pie shell. Garnish with cool whip.

Ginny Sims Craft

French Coconut Pie

2 eggs	1 teaspoon vanilla
1¼ cups sugar	½ stick butter
1 small can evaporated milk	1 can Angel flake Bakers Coconut

Cream eggs and sugar. Melt butter and mix with sugar and eggs. Add milk and vanilla. Stir in ¾ cup coconut. Put in 9-inch uncooked pie shell. Sprinkle rest of coconut on top. Cook at 350° for 45 to 60 minutes.

Ginny Sims Craft

Praline Sauce

1 cup light brown sugar	2 tablespoons butter
2½ tablespoons cornstarch	½ cup chopped pecans
1½ cups water	

In small saucepan, combine brown sugar and cornstarch. Add water and cook, stirring constantly over medium heat until thick and bubbly, about 5 minutes. Add butter stirring until melted. Stir in pecans.

Makes about 2 cups

Serve over ice cream pie.

Caramel Sauce

1 cup light brown sugar	2 tablespoons heavy cream
½ cup butter	½ teaspoon vanilla
½ cup light corn syrup	⅛ teaspoon salt

In a small heavy, non-aluminum saucepan, combine brown sugar and ¼ cup butter. Bring to a boil over moderate heat. Whisk in the corn syrup, cream, vanilla and salt. Reduce the heat to low and boil gently for about 3 minutes, stirring constantly. Immediately remove from heat and whisk in the remaining ¼ cup butter. Serve warm or at room temperature. Can store in refrigerator up to 4 months.

PNG *Chocolate Sauce*

4	squares of unsweetened chocolate (or 12 tablespoons Hershey cocoa)	3	cups sugar
½	cup margarine (1 stick)		Pinch salt
		1	large can evaporated milk
		1	teaspoon vanilla

Mix all ingredients in double boiler. Cook until thick using a whisk to stir. When done add vanilla.

Linda Sims

Terry Barnes gave me this recipe while on the mission field in Papua New Guinea.

Fudge Sauce

8	squares unsweetened baking chocolate	½	teaspoon salt
1½	cups water	¼	cup butter
2	cups sugar	1	teaspoon vanilla

Combine chocolate and water in saucepan and cook over low heat, stirring constantly until chocolate is melted and mixture is smooth. Add sugar and salt. Cook and stir about 5 minutes, or until sugar is dissolved and mixture is slightly thickened. Add butter and stir until melted. Remove from heat and add vanilla.

Makes 1 quart

Lindy Warrick, Williamsburg, Virginia

The daintiness and yet elegance of a china tea cup focuses one to be gentle, to think warmly and to feel close.

~Carol and Malcolm Cohen

Index

Index

D

Index

Index

Index

R

S

Tea Treasures
2406 Rollingwood Drive
Austin, TX 78746

Please send _____ copy(ies)   @ $19.95 each _____

        Postage and handling   @ $ 5.00 each _____

        Texas residents add 8.25% tax   @ $ 1.65 each _____

                               TOTAL _____

Name _____

Address _____

City _____ State _____ Zip _____

Make checks payable to ***Tea Treasures***.

Tea Treasures
2406 Rollingwood Drive
Austin, TX 78746

Please send _____ copy(ies)   @ $19.95 each _____

        Postage and handling   @ $ 5.00 each _____

        Texas residents add 8.25% tax   @ $ 1.65 each _____

                               TOTAL _____

Name _____

Address _____

City _____ State _____ Zip _____

Make checks payable to ***Tea Treasures***.

Tea Treasures
2406 Rollingwood Drive
Austin, TX 78746

Please send _____ copy(ies)   @ $19.95 each _____

        Postage and handling   @ $ 5.00 each _____

        Texas residents add 8.25% tax   @ $ 1.65 each _____

                               TOTAL _____

Name _____

Address _____

City _____ State _____ Zip _____

Make checks payable to ***Tea Treasures***.